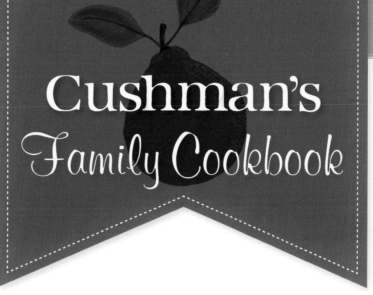

Cushman's Family Cookbook

Recipes That Celebrate
A Tradition of Uncommon Fruit Since 1945

Allen Cushman

Cushman's
Fine Citrus by Harry & David

EGG&DART™

Published by Egg & Dart™, a division of Dynamic Housewares Inc
Copyright 2011 by Dynamic Housewares Inc
All rights reserved.
Including the right of reproduction in whole or in part in any form.

Cushman's Fruit Company is a DBA of Harry and David

10 9 8 7 6 5 4 3 2 1

First paperback edition 2011

Author:

Allen Cushman

Book Design, Food Photographs, and Fruit Paintings:
Christian and Elise Stella

Copy Editor:
Kelly Machamer

Manufactured in the USA

ISBN 978-0-9841887-7-2

Contents

Fine fruit has been a Cushman family affair since the 1940s. That's when my father, Ed Cushman, opened his first citrus store in South Florida. A small place in downtown West Palm Beach, it was his pride and joy. While the real estate might have been small, his ideas were anything but.

As Floridians, we knew and loved our state's fine citrus, but for many people living elsewhere at the time, a trip down south was the only way to get your hands on sweet, ripe Florida sunshine. It was in my father's small store that he had his big idea—he would ship Florida citrus all over the country.

By 1950, my father had not only a store but his very own citrus packing plant. When my brothers, Mike and John, and I were old enough, we began to pitch in—working in the store on Saturdays and throughout the summer. Eventually, we worked right alongside our father in the packing plant. We all ate grapefruit for breakfast in the exact same way that the growers ate it—ice-cold, cut in half, and sprinkled with SALT, not sugar! Then we'd watch the fruit come in. Picked that very morning, we shipped it out in the same afternoon.

As my brothers and I got older, we joined my father in the business as partners and Cushman's Fruit Company thrived. While it was my father's idea to ship fresh Florida citrus that got our company off of the ground, it was one spectacular fruit that truly made Cushman's a household name.

While my father didn't invent the HoneyBell, he did give it its name. A hybrid between a Dancy Tangerine and Duncan Grapefruit, the HoneyBell is unlike any fruit on the planet! As sweet as honey and tapered like a bell, my father couldn't have given it a better name. Only harvested for a few short weeks in January, the HoneyBell became not only one of the most prized fruits but also the rarest. We simply refuse to pick them any other time than when they are at their ripest, most delicious peak.

Today, nearly 70 years after my father first opened his first store, Cushman's is now a proud part of the Harry and David family. It's a partnership that has allowed us to spread the joy of HoneyBells, along with plenty of other fine fruits, to more people than ever before. Through it all, we still have a storefront in South Florida and you can still find me there shaking salt on an ice-cold half of grapefruit.

It's always been an honor to bring you the juiciest, most delicious fruit in the world. Now, I am quite humbled to bring you this collection of my family's favorite recipes. You simply cannot work around fresh fruit for over half a decade without coming up with a few good dishes to make with it. More than anything, this book is for my mother. My father always knew the perfect moment to pick a perfectly ripe HoneyBell, but my mother was the one who knew what to cook with it.

-Allen Cushman

The Finest Fruit

HoneyBells

Season's Peak: January

Available for only a few short weeks in January, HoneyBells are the sweetest, most cherished citrus fruit around.

Crown Ruby Red Grapefruits

Season's Peak: Winter

Carefully grown and selected in Florida, Crown Ruby Red Grapefruits are quite simply the best in the world.

Royal Riviera Pears

Season's Peak: Fall – Early Winter

(available spring and summer too!)

With a sublime flavor, creamy texture, and lush juiciness, Royal Riviera Pears are truly unique.

Golden Pineapples

Season's Peak: Spring

Less acidic and more sweet, Golden Pineapples are a refreshingly luscious trip to the tropics.

Oregold Peaches

Season's Peak: August

Rare and indescribably juicy, these are the most highly prized and sought-after peaches grown.

Honeycrisp Apples

Season's Peak: October

These crisp, sweet, and juicy dessert apples are a delight to everyone who tries them.

Cherry-Oh!! Cherries

Season's Peak: February

Each one is a dark and delicious jewel. These sweet and crunchy dessert cherries are picked at the perfect moment.

While I am most often asked for recipes for Cushman's world famous HoneyBells, I decided early on in the process of compiling recipes for this book that I would include recipes for a variety of delicious fruits. With the short January season of HoneyBells, I wanted to be sure that this book would not only find a place in your kitchen but also find itself useful all twelve months of the year. As we only pick our fruit at the peak of ripeness, I have tried to pick a variety of fruits with a wide variety of availabilities.

The recipes in this book were specifically written for the variety of fruits they are categorized under and will come out best when made with those particular varieties. That being said, Cushman's and Harry and David sell a wide variety of delicious fruit all year round that can be substituted in these recipes if a particular variety is not in season. For instance, while Royal Riviera Pears are arguably the most delicious pears in the world, our other varieties of pears can be substituted if necessary.

The unique characteristics of different varieties of pears, apples, etc. can actually bring something new to the recipes in this book, and I encourage you to prepare them with whichever variety is in season at the time. Most of all, I encourage you to prepare the recipes in this book often!

HoneyBells are the trickiest fruit in this book to find a substitute for. There just aren't any substitutions for a sweet, juicy HoneyBell! Oranges or tangerines can be used in these recipes, but keep in mind—There just aren't any substitutions for a sweet, juicy HoneyBell! Substituting oranges in a HoneyBell recipe will lack some of the tangy, more tangerine characteristics of the HoneyBell, and substituting tangerines in these recipes may provide too much of that characteristic. As a Florida boy I love all citrus, and have made many of the HoneyBell recipes in this book with other varieties of citrus with great and unique results.

The most important thing to remember is that seasonality is key. You will get the best results from the recipes in this book when using ripe fruit at the peak of their season.

Tis' the Season

Cooking with fresh fruit can present a few challenges that are best solved with simple kitchen tools that are available in most superstores. While most of the items on this list are not necessary to create the recipes in this book, but they will definitely cut down on your preparation time.

Citrus Zester

This slender tool with sharpened round holes at the end is an absolute necessity when cooking with citrus. You simply scrape it across the rind of citrus to pull strands of zest away from the fruit. For even more flavor, I suggest you always chop the strands into even finer pieces before adding them to a recipe.

Citrus Reamer

A citrus reamer or juicer is a necessity if you want to be sure that you are getting all of the juice out of your citrus.

Fruit Peeler

A fruit and vegetable peeler is another necessity. You most likely already have one, but if it is a little dated, you would be surprised by how much of a difference purchasing a new one can make. They tend to get very dull after a few years.

Apple Corer

An apple corer is basically a handle with a hollow, tubular blade that you stick down into an apple to remove the core and seeds. Coring an apple without one is not easy or recommended! These also work very well with pears.

Apple Wedger

This nifty little device has two handles and several blades in the center that core and cut an apple into 8 wedges all in one motion! Also works well with peaches.

Pineapple Corer

There are several nifty tools available now for coring (and sometimes even peeling and slicing) fresh pineapples. Having one is highly recommended!

Cherry Pitter

Pitting fresh cherries is a task that is all but impossible without the use of this little device. As you squeeze the handle, a little metal shaft pushes the pit right out of the cherry.

Vitamin C Powder

While this one may seem strange, it is actually the best tip you will find in this book! In most grocery stores or superstores (near the pickling and jarring supplies) you will find a shaker of a powder called Fruit-Fresh Produce Protector by Ball brand. It uses vitamin C to keep fruit from oxidizing and turning brown after being cut. For the best looking dishes, I recommend sprinkling this on apples, pears, and peaches as soon as they are cut. It even works wonders on avocadoes!

Otherwise, you will want to toss these fruits in a small amount of lemon juice to keep them from oxidizing, but using lemon juice will affect the flavor of the final dish.

Honey Bells

Appetizers, Snacks, and Beverages

Breakfast and Lunches

Main Courses and Sides

Desserts

Butternut and HoneyBell Soup

TOTAL PREPARATION TIME: 1 HOUR   DIFFICULTY: EASY   SERVES: 6

Creamy and warm butternut squash soup is the perfect dish for a cold January day in HoneyBell season. Adding a touch of HoneyBell to this classic soup is a surefire way to bring a little sunshine into winter!

Shopping List

2 tablespoons butter or margarine

1 small yellow onion, diced

1 teaspoon minced garlic

5 cups diced raw butternut squash

4 cups vegetable broth

1 cup HoneyBell juice

1 teaspoon grated HoneyBell zest

2 teaspoons fresh chopped oregano

2 teaspoons sugar

¼ teaspoon salt

6 ounces plain yogurt

1 Place butter, onion, and garlic in a stock pot over medium-high heat and cook 5 minutes, or until onions begin to brown.

2 Add all remaining ingredients, except yogurt, to the stock pot and stir to combine.

3 Bring up to a boil and then reduce heat to medium-low. Cover and let simmer 30 minutes.

4 Remove from heat and let soup cool at least 20 minutes.

5 Using a handheld blender, purée soup until it is a nice, smooth consistency. You can also do this by transferring to a regular blender in as many batches as necessary.

6 Return the puréed soup to medium-high heat, cooking just until hot. Serve hot, topped with a dollop of plain yogurt.

Cushman's Tips

*Y*ou can also make a Carrot and HoneyBell Soup with 5 cups of sliced carrots in place of the butternut squash.

HoneyBell Marinated Chicken Skewers

TOTAL PREPARATION TIME: 30 MINS   **DIFFICULTY: EASY**   **SERVES: 4**

Like any food that comes on a stick, chicken skewers make a great party food! Marinated in a slightly sweet but mostly tangy HoneyBell marinade, these are so good that you'll probably want to make at least a double batch of them for your next party!

Shopping List

juice and pulp of 1 large HoneyBell

2 tablespoons soy sauce

1 tablespoon light brown sugar

1 pound boneless, skinless chicken breasts

bamboo skewers

1 In a sauce pan, simmer HoneyBell juice over medium-high heat for 5 minutes, or until reduced by about ⅓.

2 Add soy sauce and brown sugar to the reduced juice and stir to combine. Place in freezer for 10 minutes to cool down.

3 Slice chicken breasts into ¾ inch wide strips and add to the cooled marinade. Let marinate, refrigerated, for at least 2 hours.

4 Meanwhile, place bamboo skewers in a shallow dish of water to soak until ready to prepare skewers.

5 Thread the marinated chicken strips onto the soaked bamboo skewers and grill on a preheated grill or indoor grill pan over high-heat. Grill 3-4 minutes on each side, or until slicing into one reveals no pink. Serve immediately.

Cushman's Tips

These skewers are also great served over a salad or even as a replacement for the regular grilled chicken in my Grilled Chicken Salad with HoneyBell Supremes, recipe page: 27.

HoneyBell Glazed Nuts

TOTAL PREPARATION TIME: 40 MINS   DIFFICULTY: EASY   SERVES: 8

These glazed nuts have the essence of HoneyBells baked right in! I like to bake up a batch or two as thank-you gifts after the holidays and send them out in tins tied with ribbon.

Shopping List

1 large egg white

½ cup light brown sugar

⅓ cup sugar

1 tablespoon HoneyBell juice

1 packed tablespoon finely grated HoneyBell zest

1 teaspoon vanilla extract

1 teaspoon ground cinnamon

¼ teaspoon salt

1 ½ cups pecan halves

1 ½ cups raw almonds

1 Preheat oven to 300 degrees F. Line a sheet pan with parchment paper.

2 In a mixing bowl, whisk together all ingredients, except pecans and almonds, to create the glaze.

3 Gently fold pecans and almonds into the glaze and then spread out onto the parchment paper-lined sheet pan.

4 Bake 26-30 minutes, or until glaze looks crispy and you can smell the pecans roasting. Let cool 15 minutes before breaking apart to serve.

Cushman's Tips

You can use any combination of nuts to make this recipe, but they are better when you start with them raw, which can sometimes be hard to find. Cashews are really, really good when made this way but are only available raw in a few select stores.

HoneyBell Barbecue Chicken Wings

TOTAL PREPARATION TIME: **1** HOUR   DIFFICULTY: EASY   SERVES: 4-6

Chicken wings are one of my favorite appetizers, especially when they are in a tangy-sweet barbecue sauce like the one in this recipe. Just be sure to grab extra napkins!

Shopping List

2 pounds chicken wings, wing and leg separated

1 cup bottled barbecue sauce

¼ cup ketchup

2 teaspoons Worcestershire sauce

1 tablespoon honey

1 tablespoon HoneyBell zest

2 teaspoons minced garlic

1 Add chicken wings to a large dish and cover with all remaining ingredients. Toss to fully combine and coat wings.

2 Cover dish and refrigerate for at least 1 hour to marinate.

Grilling Wings

Oil and preheat a grill, indoor grill, or grill pan to medium-high. Remove wings from the dish of marinade and grill 7-9 minutes on each side, cooking until mostly white throughout.

Baking Wings

Preheat oven to 375 degrees F. Bake wings directly in the marinade for about 1 hour, or until mostly white throughout.

Cushman's Tips

I find that the ketchup adds a nice tanginess to these, but you can substitute another ¼ cup of barbecue sauce if you wish.

Strawberry, Banana, and HoneyBell Smoothies

TOTAL PREPARATION TIME: **15** MINS   DIFFICULTY: EASY   SERVES: **2**

Fresh fruit smoothies are nearly a daily indulgence in my house. With so much fruit around, is that any wonder? This is a delicious HoneyBell twist on the classic orange, strawberry, and banana combination that everyone knows and loves.

Shopping List

1 banana, peeled

¾ cup strawberries, hulls removed

1 cup HoneyBell juice, chilled

¼ teaspoon finely grated HoneyBell zest

1 tablespoon light brown sugar

1 Slice banana and place, along with strawberries, into the freezer until frozen solid.

2 Place frozen banana slices, frozen strawberries, HoneyBell juice, HoneyBell zest, and brown sugar in a blender.

3 Blend until drink is entirely smooth, about 2 minutes. Serve immediately.

Cushman's Tips

Store-bought frozen strawberries will work just fine in this recipe, but you should definitely freeze your own fresh banana. They are best frozen on a parchment paper-lined plate, otherwise the banana slices will just freeze into one large clump.

Fresh HoneyBell Soda Fountain Floats

TOTAL PREPARATION TIME: 10 MINS   DIFFICULTY: EASY   SERVES: 1

This simple HoneyBell float with vanilla ice cream is made with fresh-squeezed HoneyBell juice and just a splash of lemon-lime soda for fizz. The real secret though is a small pinch of HoneyBell zest, which gives you a much more concentrated HoneyBell taste that you simply can't get from juice alone.

Shopping List

⅔ cup HoneyBell juice, chilled

1 small pinch finely grated HoneyBell zest

⅓ cup lemon-lime soda, chilled

2 large or 3 small scoops vanilla ice cream

1 Place a large, thick glass in the freezer for at least 10 minutes to chill before preparing.

2 Pour HoneyBell juice into the chilled glass and add HoneyBell zest, stirring well.

3 Pour lemon-lime soda into the juice and then top with 2-3 scoops of vanilla ice cream. Serve immediately. Repeat all to make additional floats.

Cushman's Tips

The zest used in this recipe should be very, very finely grated and only a very small amount is needed… about ⅛ of a teaspoon.

HoneyBell and Strawberry Wine Spritzers

TOTAL PREPARATION TIME: 10 MINS   DIFFICULTY: EASY   SERVES: 1

Similar to a mimosa, this is a wonderful brunch-time HoneyBell refreshment made even more refreshing by the addition of a macerated strawberry. While I suggest making this with a nice sweet Riesling, feel free to use any white wine you wish! You can even use a fruity red table wine for a spritzer that is similar to sangria.

Shopping List

½ cup HoneyBell juice, chilled

¼ cup Riesling wine, chilled

¼ cup club soda, chilled

1 large strawberry, crushed

1 Pour chilled HoneyBell juice, Riesling, and club soda into a wine glass.

2 Stir a crushed strawberry into the wine spritzer and serve immediately.

Cushman's Tips

This is best when ice cold, so feel free to add ice cubes if needed!

Lemon-lime soda can be used in place of the club soda for a sweeter drink.

HoneyBell Glazed Cocktail Smokies

TOTAL PREPARATION TIME: 10 MINS   **DIFFICULTY: EASY**   **SERVES: 8**

Many people make sweet, glazed cocktail sausages like these with grape jelly or orange marmalade, but I make my glaze from scratch using fresh HoneyBell juice and zest. The whole dish, glaze and all, is cooked up and ready for your party in only 4 minutes in the microwave.

Shopping List

1 (16-ounce) package cocktail wieners

¾ cup light brown sugar

¼ cup HoneyBell juice

2 teaspoons HoneyBell zest

2 tablespoons Dijon mustard

1 tablespoon all-purpose flour

1 Place cocktail wieners in a microwave-safe bowl.

2 Whisk together all remaining ingredients and pour over cocktail wieners in bowl.

3 Cover bowl with plastic wrap and poke a small hole to vent. Microwave on high for 4 minutes, stirring halfway through.

4 Stir well and serve hot.

Cushman's Tips

Be sure to purchase toothpicks to put out alongside these, as the glaze can get quite hot and is definitely not something you want to grab with your fingers!

HoneyBells

Grilled Chicken Salad with HoneyBell Supremes

TOTAL PREPARATION TIME: 30 MINS   DIFFICULTY: EASY   SERVES: 4

This salad is a simple but delicious lunchtime option with an amazing HoneyBell and Poppy Seed Vinaigrette. While the recipe starts with raw chicken breasts, you can also save time by purchasing pre-cooked grilled chicken strips.

Shopping List

4 boneless, skinless chicken breasts
1 tablespoon olive oil
¼ teaspoon salt
⅛ teaspoon pepper
⅛ teaspoon garlic powder
1 bag fancy lettuce mix
2 HoneyBells, peeled and segmented
2 stalks celery, sliced
1 cup grape tomatoes
½ red onion, thinly sliced

HONEYBELL POPPY VINAIGRETTE

¼ cup HoneyBell juice
2 tablespoons red wine vinegar
1 tablespoon olive oil
1 tablespoon honey
1 teaspoon finely grated HoneyBell zest
1 teaspoon poppy seeds
¼ teaspoon salt

1 In a mixing bowl, toss together chicken breasts, olive oil, salt, pepper, and garlic powder.

2 Preheat a grill, an indoor grill, or a grill pan to high. Place chicken on grill and grill until cooked through, 4-6 minutes on each side. Let rest 5 minutes before slicing each breast.

3 Split the lettuce mix equally between 4 bowls.

4 Top the lettuce in each bowl with an equal amount of the HoneyBell segments, celery, tomatoes, and sliced onion.

5 Top each salad with a sliced chicken breast.

6 In a mixing bowl, whisk together all HoneyBell Poppy Vinaigrette ingredients and drizzle over each salad.

Cushman's Tips

You can serve the chicken in this salad warm or chilled, whichever is your preference.

HoneyBell Chicken Salad with Cashews

TOTAL PREPARATION TIME: 15 MINS   **DIFFICULTY: EASY**   **SERVES: 4**

This creamy chicken salad with tangy/sweet HoneyBell zest and crunchy cashews goes great in between 2 slices of whole grain bread or stuffed into a whole grain pita pocket. Once you've zested the HoneyBell to make this, why not peel it and serve wedges alongside your sandwich for a healthy and fresh side dish?

Shopping List

⅓ cup mayonnaise (may use light)

2 teaspoons Dijon mustard

½ teaspoon honey

1 teaspoon HoneyBell zest

½ teaspoon salt

¼ teaspoon pepper

2 cups cooked chicken, chopped

1 stalk celery, diced

¼ cup cashews, chopped

1 In a mixing bowl, combine mayonnaise, Dijon mustard, honey, HoneyBell zest, salt, and pepper to create the dressing.

2 Gently fold chicken, celery, and cashews into the dressing mixture.

3 For best taste, refrigerate for 30 minutes to let the flavors combine. Serve in sandwiches or atop a bed of lettuce garnished with supremes of HoneyBell.

Cushman's Tips

I make the best chicken salad from the pre-cooked grocery store rotisserie chickens, but you can also prepare your own cooked chicken. This is especially good when made from the dark-meat leg quarters which are almost always sold in inexpensive value packs.

HoneyBells

Cranberry HoneyBell Muffins

TOTAL PREPARATION TIME: 35 MINS   DIFFICULTY: MEDIUM   SERVES: 12

The flavors in these muffins are definitely a new and unique combination that is both sweet and tangy. With both HoneyBell juice and zest you get 12 muffins that are packed with HoneyBell flavor using only 1 actual HoneyBell.

Shopping List

DRY INGREDIENTS

2 cups all-purpose flour

⅔ cup sugar

½ teaspoon baking soda

2 teaspoons baking powder

¼ teaspoon salt

WET INGREDIENTS

1 large egg, beaten

½ cup HoneyBell juice

½ cup milk

4 tablespoons butter or margarine, melted

⅔ cup sweetened dried cranberries

2 teaspoons finely grated HoneyBell zest

½ teaspoon vanilla extract

1 Preheat oven to 375 degrees F. In a large mixing bowl, combine all Dry Ingredients, tossing well.

2 In a separate mixing bowl, combine all Wet Ingredients. Let sit 10 minutes to soften the cranberries.

3 Pour the Wet Ingredients into the Dry Ingredients, stirring all to combine into a batter.

4 Pour batter into 12 greased or paper-lined muffin cups and bake 20-22 minutes, or until a toothpick inserted into a muffin comes out clean.

Cushman's Tips

If you would prefer, you can also make these muffins without the dried cranberries for regular HoneyBell muffins.

Caribbean Turkey Burgers with HoneyBell Mayo

TOTAL PREPARATION TIME: 30 MINS   **DIFFICULTY:** EASY   **SERVES:** 4

These lean turkey burgers are seasoned with island spices and then topped with a tangy HoneyBell Mayo for an interesting, tropical take on the classic burger.

Shopping List

1 pound lean ground turkey

1 large egg white

¼ cup breadcrumbs

1 tablespoon HoneyBell juice

1 tablespoon Jamaican jerk or Caribbean seasoning

¼ cup finely diced red bell pepper

buns and burger fixings

HONEYBELL MAYO

½ cup mayonnaise

1 tablespoon HoneyBell juice

¾ teaspoon finely grated HoneyBell zest

1 In a mixing bowl, combine ground turkey, egg white, breadcrumbs, Honey-Bell juice, Caribbean seasoning, and red bell pepper.

2 Form turkey mixture into 4 large burger patties.

3 Preheat a grill, an indoor grill, or a grill pan to high. Grill turkey burgers for 6-7 minutes on each side, or until cutting into one reveals no pink.

4 In a mixing bowl, combine all Hon-eyBell Mayo ingredients.

5 Serve burgers on buns with your favorite fixings and smothered with the HoneyBell mayo.

Cushman's Tips

You can make your own Caribbean seasoning by combining ½ teaspoon dried thyme, ½ teaspoon turmeric, ⅛ teaspoon cayenne pepper, ¼ teaspoon paprika, ¼ teaspoon black pepper, ¼ teaspoon allspice, ½ teaspoon salt, ¼ teaspoon garlic powder, and ¼ teaspoon onion powder.

Homemade HoneyBell Marmalade

TOTAL PREPARATION TIME: 3 HRS   **DIFFICULTY: HARD**   **SERVES: 36**

HoneyBells make the most wonderful marmalade that is sweet and not overbearingly acidic. This recipe makes about 3 jars worth, but it is easily doubled if you have a big enough pot to cook it in. Now we can finally enjoy HoneyBells all year round!

Shopping List

3 large HoneyBells

1 large lemon

6 cups water

6 cups sugar

1 Thinly slice the HoneyBells and lemon, peel and all. Remove any seeds. Thinly slice the slices to create thin strips. Add all thin strips to a large stock pot as you work along with any juices from your cutting board.

2 Add water to the stock pot and heat over high heat until boiling. Boil 5 minutes and remove from heat.

3 Stir in sugar until fully dissolved. Cover pot and let rest at least 12 hours.

4 Uncover and place the pot back over high heat and bring back up to a boil. Reduce the heat to low and let simmer 2 hours.

5 Raise the heat to medium and cook 20 minutes, or until a kitchen thermometer registers 220 degrees F. Let cool slightly before skimming off any foam and pouring into jars. Refrigerate marmalade in sealed jars, which will keep for up to 1 year without any additional canning procedures.

Cushman's Tips

The marmalade should be a rich orange color when it is finished but not brown, so watch the thermometer carefully to ensure that the sugars do not burn.

HoneyBell Pecan Rolls

TOTAL PREPARATION TIME: 2 HRS   DIFFICULTY: HARD   SERVES: 12

Pecan rolls are a southern favorite that are most closely related to cinnamon buns. Filled with chopped pecans and HoneyBell zest, I'd take these over the plain ol' cinnamon bun any day!

Shopping List

1 (.25-ounce) envelope active dry yeast

1 cup milk, warmed

2 large eggs

6 tablespoons butter, melted

3 ½ cups all-purpose flour

1 cup Bisquick baking mix

1 cup light brown sugar

½ teaspoon salt

FILLING

4 tablespoons butter, softened

1 cup dark brown sugar

2 teaspoons ground cinnamon

2 tablespoons HoneyBell zest

1 cup chopped pecans

1 Stir yeast into the warm milk and let sit 15 minutes.

2 In a large mixing bowl, whisk together eggs and butter. Add yeast mixture, flour, Bisquick, brown sugar, and salt and knead all into a ball of dough. Cover and place in a warm place to rise for 1 hour.

3 On a floured surface, roll out dough until it is a large oval, about ½ inch thick.

4 In a mixing bowl, combine all Filling ingredients and spread over top the entire surface of the rolled out dough.

5 Roll the dough into a long pinwheel and then cut into thick slices, about 1 ½ inches thick. Place the slices, edge to edge, in a greased baking dish. Cover baking dish and let rise an additional 30 minutes.

6 Preheat oven to 400 degrees F. Uncover baking dish and bake 18-20 minutes or until rolls have puffed up and filling is bubbly hot.

Cushman's Tips

You can also make a quick icing to top these by combining 1 cup confectioners sugar, 1 ½ tablespoons milk, and ⅛ teaspoon vanilla extract. Microwave for 30 seconds and then drizzle over top rolls.

HoneyBell Beef Stir Fry

TOTAL PREPARATION TIME: **25** MINS   DIFFICULTY: EASY   SERVES: **4**

The sweet and tangy flavors of a fresh HoneyBell work extremely well in Asian dishes like this HoneyBell Beef Stir Fry. Simply serve over white or brown rice for a complete dinner.

Shopping List

1 pound top round steaks, cut into strips

¼ cup soy sauce

1 tablespoon sesame oil

1 tablespoon honey

1 tablespoon light brown sugar

2 teaspoons minced garlic

2 teaspoons HoneyBell zest

1 tablespoon vegetable oil

1 tablespoon butter or margarine

1 yellow onion, thinly sliced

2 cups snow peas

1 cup julienned carrots

⅓ cup HoneyBell juice

2 teaspoons cornstarch

1 Place steak strips, soy sauce, sesame oil, honey, brown sugar, garlic, and HoneyBell zest in a food storage container and refrigerate for at least 2 hours to marinate.

2 Place vegetable oil in a very large skillet or wok over medium-high heat. Remove beef from marinade (reserving marinade) and add to the pan. Sau-té until meat begins to brown, about 4 minutes.

3 Add butter and onions and continue sautéing for 2 minutes.

4 Add snow peas, carrots, and the reserved marinade to the skillet and cover. Let cook 2 minutes.

5 Whisk cornstarch into the Honey-Bell juice and add to the skillet. Stir to combine and cook an additional 2 minutes, just until the stir fry has thickened.

Cushman's Tips

This can also be made with strips of chicken in place of the beef.

HoneyBell and Thyme Roasted Chicken

TOTAL PREPARATION TIME: 2 HRS   **DIFFICULTY: MEDIUM**   **SERVES: 8**

I love rotisserie chicken but I don't exactly own my own rotisserie. Thankfully, I find that this roasting preparation can be just as good. Not only does the meat come out moist and juicy but also entirely infused with the great flavors of HoneyBell and thyme.

Shopping List

1 whole chicken (about 5 pounds)

1 HoneyBell, quartered

2 cloves garlic

1 sprig fresh thyme

2 tablespoons butter, melted

salt and pepper

1 teaspoon fresh thyme leaves

1 tablespoon honey

2 teaspoons finely grated HoneyBell zest

1 Preheat oven to 425 degrees F.

2 Place chicken in a roasting pan and stuff with the HoneyBell quarters, garlic, and sprig of thyme.

3 Drizzle melted butter over the entire surface of the chicken and then season with a generous amount of salt and pepper. Sprinkle the fresh thyme leaves over top.

4 Bake for 1 hour and 15 minutes.

5 Remove chicken from oven and brush with a thin coating of honey. Sprinkle the HoneyBell zest over top, letting it stick into the honey.

6 Return to the oven and bake an additional 15 minutes, or until a meat thermometer inserted into the thigh registers 175 degrees F.

Cushman's Tips

For a nice presentation, thinly slice a HoneyBell, peel and all, and overlap a few slices atop the chicken after applying the honey and zest in step 6.

Cilantro and HoneyBell Pork Chops

TOTAL PREPARATION TIME: **30** MINS   DIFFICULTY: EASY   SERVES: **4-6**

Cilantro is a wonderful fresh herb used in many Mexican dishes. It pairs extremely well with the acidic qualities of fruit, especially citrus, making for a perfect marinade for these pork chops.

Shopping List

2 pounds boneless pork loin chops

2 tablespoons olive oil

¼ cup HoneyBell juice

2 teaspoons finely grated HoneyBell zest

¼ cup fresh cilantro leaves, chopped

2 teaspoons minced garlic

¼ teaspoon salt

⅛ teaspoon pepper

1 Add pork chops to a large bowl and cover with olive oil, HoneyBell juice, HoneyBell zest, cilantro, garlic, salt, and pepper. Toss to fully coat, cover bowl, and refrigerate for 1 hour to marinate.

2 Remove pork chops from marinade and grill or pan-fry before serving alongside your favorite sides.

Grilling Pork Chops

Oil and preheat a grill, indoor grill, or grill pan to medium-high. Grill pork chops 3-10 minutes on each side, just until well-marked and mostly white throughout. Thin chops (¼-inch thick) should take 3-4 minutes on each side to cook. Thick chops (¾-inch thick) should take about 10 minutes on each side.

Pan-frying Pork Chops

Place chops in a large skillet over medium-high heat. Cook 3-4 minutes on each side, until browned. For thin chops (¼-inch thick) they should be done. For thick chops (¾-inch thick) you should transfer the browned chops to an oven preheated at 400 degrees F. and bake 10 minutes, or until chops are mostly white throughout.

HoneyBell Glazed Ham

TOTAL PREPARATION TIME: 2+ HRS   DIFFICULTY: EASY   SERVES: 16

Pre-glazed hams are convenient but can cost quite a lot more than simply creating the glaze yourself! Besides that, when you're making your own glaze, you can do something pretty amazing... like make a glaze out of sweet and delicious HoneyBells!

Shopping List

1 bone-in cured ham

1 teaspoon cornstarch

½ cup HoneyBell juice

¼ cup honey

1 cup light brown sugar

2 tablespoons Dijon mustard

1 tablespoon HoneyBell zest

1 Preheat oven to 325 degrees F. Check ham package for weight before unwrapping.

2 Place ham in a roasting pan and bake for 15 minutes per pound of weight.

3 Meanwhile, whisk cornstarch into the HoneyBell juice and add to a sauce pot over medium-high heat.

4 Whisk all remaining ingredients into the pot and bring up to a simmer. Let simmer 4 minutes, whisking occasionally, to create the HoneyBell Glaze. Remove from heat.

5 When ham has only 30 minutes of baking time remaining, thoroughly brush with some of the HoneyBell glaze.

6 When ham has only 15 minutes of baking time remaining, brush all remaining glaze over the ham.

Cushman's Tips

*F*or a nice presentation, thinly slice a HoneyBell, peel and all, and overlap a few slices atop the ham after applying the glaze in step 5.

HoneyBell Sweet Potato Casserole

TOTAL PREPARATION TIME: 1 ½ HRS   DIFFICULTY: MEDIUM   SERVES: 8

I find Sweet Potato Casserole to be a great winter side dish in general and not just a Thanksgiving kind of thing. In my version, I start with mashed sweet potatoes and add a good amount of HoneyBell zest and chopped pecans. For me, topping this casserole with marshmallows is an absolute must.

Shopping List

2 ½ pounds sweet potatoes, peeled and cubed

nonstick cooking spray

½ cup sugar

1 large egg, beaten

¼ cup half and half

4 tablespoons butter or margarine, melted

1 tablespoon HoneyBell zest

1 teaspoon vanilla extract

¼ teaspoon ground cinnamon

⅔ cup chopped pecans

2 cups miniature marshmallows

1 Place cubed sweet potatoes into a pot of boiling water and boil until fork tender, about 10 minutes. Drain well.

2 Preheat oven to 350 degrees F. Spray a 13x9 baking dish with nonstick cooking spray.

3 Mash the cooked sweet potato cubes and cover with sugar, egg, half and half, butter, HoneyBell zest, vanilla extract, cinnamon, and pecans. Stir until all is well combined.

4 Spread sweet potato mixture into the greased baking dish and top with miniature marshmallows.

5 Bake 35-40 minutes, or until marshmallows are golden brown. Serve hot.

Cushman's Tips

If you are not a fan of the marshmallow-topped sweet potato casserole, you can also make this topped with crumbled graham crackers. Or for something more savory, you can try making this with crumbled Ritz crackers over the top.

HoneyBells

Spicy HoneyBell Sautéed Shrimp

TOTAL PREPARATION TIME: 15 MINS   DIFFICULTY: EASY   SERVES: 4

Citrus fruit is not only the perfect complement to seafood but also Asian dishes like this spicy shrimp sauté. HoneyBells work particularly well here as their natural sweetness (along with a little honey) really balances out the spicy red pepper flakes that give this dish its punch. Of course, you can also leave out the red pepper flakes for a mild take on this recipe.

Shopping List

¾ cup HoneyBell juice

1 tablespoon cornstarch

2 tablespoons soy sauce

¾ teaspoon dried red pepper flakes

1 tablespoon honey

1 ½ pounds shrimp, thawed, peeled, and deveined

½ teaspoon HoneyBell zest

1 tablespoon cornstarch

½ teaspoon salt

⅛ teaspoon pepper

⅛ teaspoon garlic powder

2 tablespoons sesame oil

sliced green onions, for garnish

1 Whisk HoneyBell juice, 1 tablespoon of cornstarch, soy sauce, red pepper flakes, and honey in a sauce pot over medium-high heat. Bring up to a simmer and let cook 2 minutes, or until thickened.

2 Meanwhile, toss shrimp in Honey-Bell zest, 1 tablespoon of cornstarch, salt, pepper, and garlic powder.

3 Heat sesame oil in a large skillet over medium-high heat for 1 minute. Add shrimp and cook for 2-3 minutes on each side, or until lightly browned.

4 Add the thickened sauce to the shrimp and toss to coat. Bring sauce back up to a simmer and then serve immediately, garnished with sliced green onion.

Cushman's Tips

This is best served over steamed white or brown rice, but it can also be served lo-mein style by tossing cooked spaghetti in with the shrimp and sauce in step 4.

HoneyBells

Buttery HoneyBell Carrots

TOTAL PREPARATION TIME: **20** MINS   DIFFICULTY: **EASY**   SERVES: **8**

Sweet and delicious glazed carrots are one of my favorite side dishes, most likely because they are a little bit like having dessert with dinner! Infusing the carrots with the taste of HoneyBells adds something entirely new to this classic dish.

Shopping List

2 pounds baby carrots

4 tablespoons butter or margarine

2 tablespoons water

2 tablespoons light brown sugar

¼ teaspoon salt

2 teaspoons finely grated HoneyBell zest

2 teaspoons cornstarch

1 Place carrots, butter, water, brown sugar, and salt in a microwave-safe bowl and cover with plastic wrap. Poke a small hole in the plastic wrap to vent.

2 Microwave on high for 10 minutes, stirring halfway through.

3 Remove plastic wrap and stir in HoneyBell zest and cornstarch. Return to microwave and heat on high 3-4 minutes, or until sauce is thickened. Serve hot.

Cushman's Tips

You can also make this on the stove in a covered sauté pan over medium heat. You will need to sauté the carrots for at least 15 minutes before adding the cornstarch to ensure that they get tender.

HoneyBell Cream Cake

TOTAL PREPARATION TIME: 1 ½ HRS   **DIFFICULTY:** EASY   **SERVES:** 12

This creamy, HoneyBell-infused cake is as rich as pound cake but easily made with boxed cake mix. Made in a large Bundt pan, this simple dessert can easily serve 12 people, so make sure you have a crowd on hand!

Shopping List

nonstick cooking spray
1 (18.25-ounce) box yellow cake mix
1 (3.4-ounce) box vanilla instant pudding mix
2 sticks butter or margarine, softened
4 large eggs
1 cup milk
1 tablespoon finely grated HoneyBell zest

ICING

1 cup confectioners sugar
1 ½ tablespoons HoneyBell juice
1 teaspoon finely grated HoneyBell zest
¼ teaspoon vanilla extract

1 Preheat oven to 325 degrees F. Spray a 12 cup Bundt pan or tube pan with nonstick cooking spray.

2 In an electric mixer, combine yellow cake mix, instant pudding mix, butter, eggs, milk, and HoneyBell zest. Beat until smooth and creamy, about 2 minutes.

3 Pour cake batter into the greased Bundt pan.

4 Bake 60-65 minutes, or until the top is puffy and browned and a toothpick inserted into the center comes out mostly clean. Let cool completely.

5 In a microwave-safe bowl, combine all Icing ingredients and microwave 30 seconds, just until mixture is smooth and somewhat thin. Drizzle evenly over the baked cake and let cool 5 minutes. Slice and serve at room temperature or chilled.

Cushman's Tips

For something a little simpler, you can skip the icing on this and simply dust the top of the cake with confectioners sugar before slicing.

HoneyBell Cheesecake Cups

TOTAL PREPARATION TIME: 45 MINS   **DIFFICULTY: MEDIUM**   **SERVES: 8-12**

Cheesecakes are typically flavored with a small hint of lemon juice, but these personal-sized cheesecake cups are absolutely bursting with HoneyBell flavor.

Shopping List

CRUST

1 cup graham cracker crumbs

4 tablespoons butter or margarine, melted

3 tablespoons sugar

FILLING

2 (8-ounce) packages cream cheese, softened

⅔ cup sugar

2 large eggs

3 tablespoons milk

1 tablespoon finely grated HoneyBell zest

¾ teaspoon vanilla extract

1 Preheat oven to 350 degrees F. Fill a large baking dish with about 1 inch of water and place in the oven to preheat.

2 In a mixing bowl, combine all Crust ingredients until mixture is thick and crumbly.

3 In an electric mixer, beat together all Filling ingredients until well combined, about 2 minutes.

4 Press an equal amount of the crust mixture into the bottom of 12 nonstick or silicone muffin cups or into 8 greased ramekins.

5 Cover crust in each cup with an equal amount of the cheesecake filling, shaking from side to side to even out the top.

6 Place muffin cups or ramekins into the preheated water bath in the oven. Bake 25-30 minutes, or until the tops have puffed up and are beginning to crack. Let cool on counter for 2 hours and then refrigerate for at least 2 more. Serve chilled.

Cushman's Tips

The perfect garnish for these cheesecake cups (as pictured at left) is my Candied HoneyBell Peel, recipe page: 56.

HoneyBell and Pistachio Cookies

TOTAL PREPARATION TIME: 25 MINS   DIFFICULTY: EASY   SERVES: 12

These delicious cookies are not only infused with the flavor of a fresh HoneyBell but are also packed with creamy pistachio nuts that are ground right into the flour. Makes about 24 regular-sized cookies that are best served warm.

Shopping List

nonstick cooking spray

1 ½ sticks butter or margarine, softened

1 cup sugar

1 large egg

¾ cup shelled pistachio nuts

2 cups all-purpose flour

1 tablespoon finely grated HoneyBell zest

1 ½ teaspoons baking powder

¼ teaspoon baking soda

1 Preheat oven to 350 degrees F. Spray 2 cookie sheets with nonstick cooking spray.

2 In an electric mixer, beat together butter, sugar, and egg.

3 Place pistachios in a food processor and pulse until very finely chopped.

4 Add chopped pistachios, flour, HoneyBell zest, baking powder, and baking soda to the butter mixture and mix until all is combined into a thick dough.

5 Place tablespoon sized balls of cookie dough on the greased cookie sheet about 3 inches apart and press down to flatten.

6 Bake 10-15 minutes, just until the edges begin to brown. Let cool 5 minutes before serving.

Cushman's Tips

Roasted and salted pistachios work perfectly in this recipe as I find that the salt really offsets the sweet cookie dough.

HoneyBell and Cream Parfaits

TOTAL PREPARATION TIME: 10 MINS   DIFFICULTY: EASY   SERVES: 4

These parfaits are made with ricotta cheese, just like the nice filling of an Italian cannoli. In fact, some stores even sell frozen cannoli shells that you can defrost and fill with this HoneyBell and ricotta cream. Personally, I think it's good enough to eat all on its own.

Shopping List

1 ¼ cups ricotta cheese

¼ cup milk

1 tablespoon vanilla instant pudding mix

2 teaspoons honey

2 teaspoons finely grated HoneyBell zest

1 In a large bowl, combine ricotta cheese, milk, instant pudding mix, honey, and HoneyBell zest. For best results, use a hand mixer, beating until smooth and fluffy.

2 Refrigerate for 1 hour to set before spooning an equal amount of the mixture into four small glasses or bowls to serve.

Cushman's Tips

For the best presentation, serve topped with a vanilla cookie and a piece of my Candied HoneyBell Peel, recipe page: 56.

HoneyBell Cookie Drops

TOTAL PREPARATION TIME: 30 MINS   **DIFFICULTY: EASY**   **SERVES: 12**

These little shortbread cookies pack more than a little bit of HoneyBell goodness. Why not pack a batch in a carton or tin and give them as a gift? You will want to make two batches if gifting, as you may find these way too good to give away!

Shopping List

nonstick cooking spray

1 stick butter or margarine, softened

¾ cup sugar

¼ cup light brown sugar

1 large egg

¼ cup sour cream

1 tablespoon finely grated HoneyBell zest

2 tablespoons HoneyBell juice

2 cups all-purpose flour

1 ½ teaspoons baking soda

⅛ teaspoon salt

1 Preheat oven to 350 degrees F. Spray 2 cookie sheets with nonstick cooking spray.

2 In an electric mixer, beat together butter, sugar, light brown sugar, egg, sour cream, HoneyBell zest, and HoneyBell juice.

3 Add flour, baking soda, and salt to the mixture and beat for about 1 minute, or until all is well combined.

4 Place teaspoon sized balls of cookie dough on the greased cookie sheet about 2 inches apart.

5 Bake 15 minutes, or until edges of cookies begin to crisp. Cool completely before serving. Makes about 48 cookie drops.

Cushman's Tips

When you first remove the cookies they will be quite soft, but they harden up as they cool.

Hint of HoneyBell Brownies

TOTAL PREPARATION TIME: 45 MINS   DIFFICULTY: EASY   SERVES: 9

I named these Hint of HoneyBell Brownies because it had a nice ring to it, but I must say that these fudgy bars have more than just a "Hint" of that HoneyBell flavor that we all know and love! Maybe I should've called them "Whole Lotta' HoneyBell Brownies"? Either way, the important thing is that they are delicious!

Shopping List

nonstick cooking spray

½ cup vegetable oil

1 cup sugar

1 tablespoon butter or margarine, softened

2 large eggs

1 tablespoon HoneyBell zest

1 teaspoon vanilla extract

½ cup unsweetened cocoa powder

½ cup all-purpose flour

¼ teaspoon baking powder

½ cup semisweet chocolate chips

1 Preheat oven to 350 degrees F. Spray an 8x8 baking dish with nonstick cooking spray.

2 In an electric mixer, beat together vegetable oil, sugar, butter, eggs, Honey-Bell zest, and vanilla extract.

3 Add cocoa powder, flour, and baking powder to the mixture and beat for about 1 minute, or until all is well combined. Gently fold in chocolate chips.

4 Pour batter into the greased baking dish and bake 25-30 minutes, or until the center is mostly set and only slightly jiggles when nudged with a potholder. Let cool at least 10 minutes before cutting into 9 squares.

Cushman's Tips

For fudgier brownies, pull them out of the oven the second they seem well set. For cake-like brownies leave them in a few more minutes.

HoneyBell and Cashew Chocolate Bark

TOTAL PREPARATION TIME: 15 MINS   DIFFICULTY: MEDIUM   SERVES: 12

I love to make chocolate bark, as the options for toppings are pretty much endless. In this particular recipe, I top semi-sweet chocolate with roasted cashew halves and sugared HoneyBell zest for the perfect combination of sweet and salty.

Shopping List

1 (12-ounce) bag semi-sweet chocolate chips

⅔ cup cashew halves

1 tablespoon HoneyBell zest

2 teaspoons sugar

1 Line a sheet pan with parchment paper.

2 Place chocolate chips in a metal or tempered-glass mixing bowl and place over a pot of simmering water to create a double boiler.

3 Heat until entirely melted, stirring the chocolate chips constantly.

4 Pour melted chocolate onto the parchment paper lined sheet pan and spread until about ⅓ inch thick.

5 In a mixing bowl, toss together cashews, HoneyBell zest, and sugar. Sprinkle mixture over the entire surface of the chocolate. Use a rubber spatula to press all down into the chocolate. Let cool completely until firm. Break apart and serve.

Cushman's Tips

Once you've melted the chocolate, it is important to work very fast or it will harden before you can get the cashews and zest to stick.

HoneyBell Cupcakes

TOTAL PREPARATION TIME: 45 MINS DIFFICULTY: MEDIUM SERVES: 24

Cupcakes are pretty popular these days, but I am proud to say that I've made these HoneyBell cupcakes for at least 2 decades! I haven't always topped them with candy (as they are in the picture), but these days you've got to take that extra step to compete!

Shopping List

1 (18.25-ounce) box yellow cake mix

3 large eggs

⅓ cup vegetable oil

¾ cup water

½ cup HoneyBell juice

2 teaspoons HoneyBell zest

FROSTING

8 ounces cream cheese, softened

1 stick butter, softened

½ teaspoon vanilla extract

1 teaspoon finely grated HoneyBell zest

1 (16-ounce) box confectioners sugar

1 Preheat oven to 350 degrees F. Line muffin pans with 24 cupcake liners.

2 In an electric mixer, combine yellow cake mix, eggs, vegetable oil, water, HoneyBell juice, and HoneyBell zest. Beat until smooth and creamy, about 2 minutes.

3 Pour cake batter into the prepared cupcake liners, filling them about ⅔ of the way full.

4 Bake 18-22 minutes, or until a toothpick inserted into the center of a cupcake comes out mostly clean. Let cool completely.

5 With an electric mixer, create the Frosting by beating the cream cheese, butter, vanilla extract, and HoneyBell zest until creamy.

6 Slowly beat in confectioners sugar until all is combined and a thick Frosting has formed. Refrigerate for 30 minutes to harden before spreading over top each of the cupcakes. If you desire, garnish with orange sprinkles and/or orange candies (as pictured at left).

Cushman's Tips

It should go without saying that a pastry bag is the best way to apply the frosting to the cupcakes.

Candied HoneyBell Peel

TOTAL PREPARATION TIME: 1 DAY   DIFFICULTY: MEDIUM   SERVES: 16+

Candied citrus peel is a delicious treat that I've enjoyed for as long as I can remember. Whether you eat them on their own or use them just to garnish other desserts, I believe that no peel candies better than HoneyBell peel!

Shopping List

peels of 4-6 HoneyBells

2 cups sugar

1 cup water

2 drops vanilla extract

parchment paper

additional sugar, to coat

1 Place large pieces of HoneyBell peel in a pot of boiling water over high heat. Boil for 30 minutes, drain, and rinse under cold water.

2 Using a butter knife, scrape the white away from the inside of the boiled peels, and then cut the large pieces of peel into thin strips, less than ¼ of an inch wide.

3 Place the 2 cups sugar, 1 cup water, and vanilla extract in a saucepot over medium-high heat. Cook, stirring constantly, until the mixture is simmering.

4 Stir in the thin strips of orange peel and reduce heat to medium-low, just high enough to keep the mixture simmering. Let simmer 10 minutes.

5 Remove mixture from heat and carefully transfer the peels out of the hot sugar mixture and onto baking sheets lined with parchment paper. Let cool, uncovered, overnight.

6 Remove candied peels from paper and toss in white sugar to coat before serving.

Cushman's Tips

This recipe is best made using a candy thermometer to insure that the sugar and water mixture is simmering at the correct temperature of 230 degrees F at all times.

HoneyBell and Caramel Sundae Sauce

TOTAL PREPARATION TIME: **15** MINS   DIFFICULTY: **EASY**   SERVES: **12**

This HoneyBell and Caramel Sundae Sauce makes not only a great ice cream topping but also a great garnish for all kinds of desserts. Try drizzling it over French toast or simply swirling it on a dessert plate before putting down a slice of cake or pie for a restaurant-quality presentation.

Shopping List

1 ¼ cups light brown sugar

1 stick butter or margarine

2 teaspoons cornstarch

½ cup half and half

2 teaspoons HoneyBell zest

1 Add brown sugar and butter to a sauce pot over medium-high heat and whisk until fully melted, combined, and bubbling.

2 Whisk cornstarch into the half and half until fully combined. Whisk mixture into the bubbling hot sugar mixture on the stove.

3 Add HoneyBell zest to the pot and continue whisking as you cook the caramel sauce for 2 additional minutes. Remove from heat and let cool.

4 Serve warm or chilled, refrigerating any unused caramel.

Cushman's Tips

This will thicken in the refrigerator but can be re-warmed by cooking in the microwave for 30 seconds if you need to thin it out to get a nice drizzle for your dessert.

White Chocolate and HoneyBell Fudge

TOTAL PREPARATION TIME: 15 MINS   DIFFICULTY: EASY   SERVES: 16

This recipe for white chocolate fudge with crunchy pecans and the essence of HoneyBell comes together in only 2 minutes in the microwave! Citrus infused fudge is a Florida tradition, especially when filled with or rolled in crunchy pecans!

Shopping List

12 ounces (about 3 cups) white chocolate chips

1 (14-ounce) can sweetened condensed milk

1 tablespoon butter or margarine

1 tablespoon HoneyBell zest

⅔ cup chopped pecans

1 Place all ingredients, except pecans, in a microwave-safe bowl.

2 Microwave on high for 30 seconds. Carefully remove and stir well.

3 Continue microwaving in 30 second intervals, stirring after each time, until chocolate is completely melted and everything is combined.

4 Fold the chopped pecans into the hot fudge and then immediately pour mixture into an 8x8 baking dish.

5 Refrigerate for 2 hours or until fudge is entirely set. Slice into squares and serve.

Cushman's Tips

A nonstick 8x8 baking dish works best as you can easily remove the fudge after cooling. If using a regular baking dish, either grease with nonstick cooking spray or line with parchment paper for best results.

Crown Ruby Red
Grapefruits

Appetizers

Cucumber, Onion, and Grapefruit Salad 62
Scallops with Grapefruit Sauce 63

Lunches

Grapefruit and Avocado Salad 65
Shrimp and Kiwi Salad with Grapefruit Dressing 66
Citrus Salad with Mint 67
Touch of Grapefruit Tuna Melts 69

Desserts

Ruby Red Grapefruit Bars 71
Mom's Broiled Grapefruit 72
Strawberry Grapefruit Italian Ice 73
Grapefruit Meringue Pie 75

Crown Ruby Red
GRAPEFRUITS

Cucumber, Onion, and Grapefruit Salad

TOTAL PREPARATION TIME: 20 MINS   **DIFFICULTY: EASY**   **SERVES: 4**

This simple marinated salad is a lot like an Italian classic but with grapefruit segments in place of the more traditional tomato wedges. It makes a very light and refreshing alternative to heavier, mayonnaise-based salads like potato or macaroni salads.

Shopping List

1 large cucumber, thinly sliced

2 grapefruits, peeled and segmented

½ red onion, thinly sliced

3 tablespoons extra virgin olive oil

1 tablespoon balsamic vinegar

2 teaspoons honey

¼ teaspoon salt

⅛ teaspoon black pepper

1 Place sliced cucumber, grapefruit segments, and sliced red onion in a large bowl.

2 In a mixing bowl, whisk together all remaining ingredients to create the dressing.

3 Pour dressing over cucumber, grapefruit, and onions and toss all to combine.

4 Cover and refrigerate for 15 minutes to marinate before serving.

Cushman's Tips

*W*hile this is best when marinated for 15-30 minutes, the cucumbers and onions will get soggy if left to marinate overnight.

Scallops with Grapefruit Sauce

TOTAL PREPARATION TIME: 15 MINS   DIFFICULTY: EASY   SERVES: 4-8

These sautéed scallops in a tangy white wine, butter, and grapefruit sauce make a great entrée but can also be served alongside fancy toothpicks as an elegant appetizer.

Shopping List

1 pound sea scallops

2 tablespoons all-purpose flour

salt and pepper

2 tablespoons olive oil

¼ cup diced red onion

¼ cup dry white wine

⅓ cup grapefruit juice

½ teaspoon grapefruit zest

3 tablespoons butter

¼ teaspoon salt

⅛ teaspoon pepper

1 Toss scallops in flour and then generously season with salt and pepper.

2 Heat oil in a large skillet over medium-high heat for 1 minute. Add scallops and sauté for 3-5 minutes, or until scallops are browned and slightly springy to the touch. Remove scallops from pan and set aside.

3 Add onions to the skillet and sauté for 1 minute, just until they begin to brown.

4 Add white wine, grapefruit juice, and grapefruit zest to the pan and bring up to a simmer. Let simmer 2 minutes.

5 Remove pan from heat and stir in butter, salt, pepper, and the reserved scallops. Stir just until butter is melted into the sauce. Serve immediately.

Cushman's Tips

This recipe is best with real butter, not margarine, as it really thickens the sauce. To cut back on fat, you can substitute light butter in place of the regular.

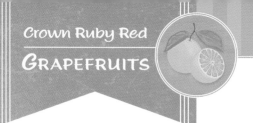

Grapefruit and Avocado Salad

TOTAL PREPARATION TIME: 20 MINS   DIFFICULTY: EASY   SERVES: 4

Avocado and grapefruit are a surprisingly good combination, especially when served over a simple salad like this one. Drizzled with a homemade grapefruit vinaigrette, this recipe makes a perfect, light lunch.

Shopping List

1 bag fancy lettuce mix

1 grapefruit, peeled and segmented

2 avocadoes, peeled, pitted, and sliced

DRESSING

¼ cup grapefruit juice

1 teaspoon Dijon mustard

2 tablespoons extra virgin olive oil

1 teaspoon minced garlic

¼ teaspoon dry oregano

¼ teaspoon salt

⅛ teaspoon pepper

1 Split the lettuce mix equally between 4 bowls.

2 Top the lettuce in each bowl with a few segments of grapefruit, and then fan ½ of an avocado across the center of each salad.

3 Create the dressing by adding all Dressing ingredients to a bowl and whisking until combined.

4 Serve each salad drizzled with the dressing.

Cushman's Tips

*W*hen making this salad, the easiest way to keep the sliced avocado from turning brown is to drizzle them with a little bit of fresh grapefruit juice as soon as you cut them.

Crown Ruby Red
GRAPEFRUITS

Shrimp and Kiwi Salad with Grapefruit Dressing

TOTAL PREPARATION TIME: 25 MINS   DIFFICULTY: MEDIUM   SERVES: 2

This tropical salad with grilled shrimp is topped with diced tomato, red onion, and fresh kiwi for a delicious change of the lunchtime pace. It is served with a simple and tart grapefruit dressing that perfectly counters the sweet kiwi fruit.

Shopping List

bamboo skewers

½ pound jumbo shrimp, peeled

1 tablespoon olive oil

salt and pepper

1 bag fancy lettuce mix

½ cup diced tomato

¼ cup diced red onion

1 kiwi, peeled and diced

DRESSING

⅓ cup grapefruit juice

1 tablespoon olive oil

1 tablespoon honey

¼ teaspoon dry oregano

⅛ teaspoon salt

1 Soak bamboo skewers in water for 30 minutes. Preheat a grill, indoor grill, or grill pan to high.

2 Toss shrimp in the olive oil and thread onto bamboo skewers, 3 per skewer. Sprinkle with a generous amount of salt and pepper.

3 Grill shrimp 3-4 minutes on each side, or until mostly white throughout. Remove from skewers and set aside.

4 Fill 2 large salad bowls with fancy lettuce mix. Top the lettuce in each bowl with an equal amount of the diced tomato, onion, and kiwi.

5 Top each salad with half of the warm grilled shrimp.

6 Whisk together all Dressing ingredients and drizzle over salads before serving.

Cushman's Tips

You can also make this salad with cantaloupe, mango, or pineapple in place of the kiwi, if desired.

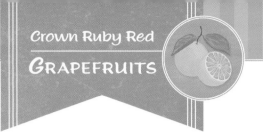
Citrus Salad with Mint

TOTAL PREPARATION TIME: **15** MINS   DIFFICULTY: EASY   SERVES: **6**

This refreshing salad combines grapefruit and orange segments with a sweet and tart honey and lemon dressing. Accented with fresh chopped mint, it's always the simplest things that bring the most pleasure!

Shopping List

2 grapefruits, peeled, seeded, and segmented

3 large oranges or HoneyBells, peeled, seeded, and segmented

zest and juice of 1 small lemon

1 tablespoon honey

2 tablespoons light brown sugar

⅛ teaspoon salt

1 sprig fresh mint, finely chopped

1 Place grapefruit and orange segments in a large bowl.

2 In a small mixing bowl, whisk together lemon zest and juice, honey, brown sugar, and salt to create the dressing.

3 Pour dressing over citrus in the large bowl and sprinkle with the fresh mint. Toss all to combine.

4 Cover and refrigerate for 15 minutes before serving chilled.

Cushman's Tips

You can also make this with lime juice and zest in place of the lemon or a combination of the two for a salad with even more fresh citrus flavor!

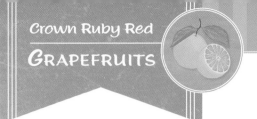

Touch of Grapefruit Tuna Melts

TOTAL PREPARATION TIME: **20** MINS   DIFFICULTY: EASY   SERVES: **4**

I've always loved a hint of citrus in my tuna salad sandwiches, but it has only been recently that I decided to try grapefruit zest in place of my usual lemon juice. Not only does it add a new and unique flavor, but using zest in place of juice also keeps the salad from getting too watered down.

Shopping List

2 (5-ounce) cans white tuna, drained

1 teaspoon finely grated grapefruit zest

⅓ cup mayonnaise

¼ cup diced yellow onion

¼ cup diced celery

2 tablespoons sweet relish

¼ teaspoon salt

⅛ teaspoon pepper

8 slices wheat, rye, or pumpernickel bread

8 thin slices tomato

4 slices Cheddar cheese

2 tablespoons butter or margarine

1 In a mixing bowl, fold together tuna, grapefruit zest, mayonnaise, onion, celery, relish, salt, and pepper to create the tuna salad.

2 Top each of 4 slices of bread with 2 slices of tomato. Place a large scoop of tuna salad over top of tomatoes on each sandwich.

3 Top each sandwich with a slice of Cheddar cheese and then the remaining slices of bread to finish.

4 Place 1 tablespoon of butter in a nonstick skillet over medium heat, heating until melted. Place two of the four sandwiches in the skillet and cook 4-5 minutes on each side, until golden brown.

5 Repeat the last step with the remaining tablespoon of butter and remaining two sandwiches. Serve each sandwich as soon as it comes out of the pan.

Cushman's Tips

Placing a lid over the skillet as you brown the sandwiches helps warm the tuna salad throughout and get the cheese melted and gooey.

Ruby Red Grapefruit Bars

TOTAL PREPARATION TIME: 50 MINS   DIFFICULTY: MEDIUM   SERVES: 10

Though these look like your ordinary lemon bars, they definitely do not taste ordinary! I love these grapefruit versions of the classic custard bars even more than the lemon ones that most people know so well.

Shopping List

1 cup all-purpose flour

¼ cup light brown sugar

1 stick butter, cold

1 pinch salt

FILLING

3 large eggs

1 cup sugar

3 tablespoons all-purpose flour

⅓ cup grapefruit juice

1 teaspoon finely grated grapefruit zest

¼ teaspoon baking powder

confectioners sugar, for garnish

1 Preheat oven to 350 degrees F. Line an 8x8 inch baking dish with parchment paper.

2 In a mixing bowl, mash together flour, light brown sugar, cold butter, and salt to create the crust. Press into the bottom of the paper-lined baking dish and bake 15 minutes.

3 In a clean mixing bowl, whisk together all Filling ingredients until well combined. Pour over the pre-baked crust.

4 Bake for 20-24 minutes, or until the custard filling is set.

5 Let cool on the counter for 2 hours before refrigerating at least 1 additional hour. Slice in half horizontally and then into 5 sections vertically to make 10 bars. Serve chilled and topped with a sprinkling of confectioners sugar for garnish.

Cushman's Tips

*Y*ou will know that the custard has set when it is beginning to brown around the edges and jiggles like gelatin.

Mom's Broiled Grapefruit

TOTAL PREPARATION TIME: **15** MINS   DIFFICULTY: EASY   SERVES: **4**

The fruit cut in half, glazed with sugar, and topped with a maraschino cherry smack dab in the middle, this is exactly how my mother used to prepare grapefruit for us. Her secret was just a tiny bit of cinnamon added to the sugar.

Shopping List

2 grapefruits

¼ cup light brown sugar

2 tablespoons sugar

¼ teaspoon cinnamon

4 maraschino cherries

1 Slice grapefruits in half and remove any seeds and the white membranes from their centers. Place the 4 halves on a sheet pan.

2 In a mixing bowl, combine brown sugar, sugar, and cinnamon.

3 Sprinkle an equal amount of the sugar mixture over each grapefruit half and then place a single maraschino cherry in the center.

4 Place an oven rack ⅓ from the top of the oven and preheat the broiler to high.

5 Place sheet pan of grapefruit halves in oven and broil for just 2-3 minutes, or until sugar is bubbling and golden brown. Serve warm.

Cushman's Tips

*Y*ou can make these a lot easier to eat by sliding a grapefruit spoon between the meat and peel of the grapefruit, loosening things up, before topping with the sugar and broiling.

Strawberry Grapefruit Italian Ice

TOTAL PREPARATION TIME: 20 MINS   DIFFICULTY: EASY   SERVES: 4-6

This Italian ice is a sweet, tart, and refreshing treat on a warm day. We have a lot of those warm days in Florida, so I know a thing or two about how refreshing this recipe can be!

Shopping List

2 cups water

1 cup sugar

¾ cup grapefruit juice

½ teaspoon grapefruit zest

8 strawberries, hulled

1 Add water and sugar to a sauce pot over medium-high heat and bring to a boil. Let cook 2 minutes.

2 Remove from heat and stir in grapefruit juice and zest. Let cool 15 minutes.

3 Place grapefruit and sugar mixture in a food processor or blender and then add strawberries. Pulse or blend until strawberries are entirely puréed into the mixture.

4 Pour the finished mixture into a food storage container or bowl, cover, and freeze until solid, at least 4 hours.

Cushman's Tips

This is easiest to eat if you pour the Italian ice base into individual serving dishes before freezing, as Italian ice isn't exactly scoopable! Serve with a heavy spoon to scrape and shave the ice out of the dish.

Grapefruit Meringue Pie

TOTAL PREPARATION TIME: **45** MINS   DIFFICULTY: **HARD**   SERVES: **8**

While Lemon Meringue Pies get all of the glory, all citrus fruit is perfectly suited for this custard and meringue treatment! Grapefruits make a particularly good meringue pie that is sweet, tart, and packed with flavor.

Shopping List

1 9-inch refrigerated pie crust, thawed

1 teaspoon all-purpose flour

1 cup sugar

3 tablespoons all-purpose flour

2 tablespoons cornstarch

1 cup water

2 tablespoons butter, melted

⅔ cup grapefruit juice

2 teaspoons finely grated grapefruit zest

5 large egg yolks

5 large egg whites

⅛ teaspoon vanilla extract

½ cup white sugar

1 Preheat oven to 350 degrees F. Press pie crust into the bottom of a 9-inch pie plate and weigh down with pie weights or dry beans. Pre-bake 15 minutes. Remove from oven, remove pie weights, and sprinkle crust with the 1 teaspoon of flour.

2 In a sauce pan over medium-high heat, whisk together 1 cup sugar, 3 table-spoons flour, cornstarch, water, butter, grapefruit juice, and zest. Bring up to a simmer and let cook 3 minutes.

3 In a mixing bowl, whisk the egg yolks. While still whisking yolks, remove a ladle of the simmering grapefruit juice mixture and whisk into the egg yolks. Next, whisk the simmering grapefruit juice as you slowly pour the (now warmed) yolk mixture into the pan until all is combined. Continue whisking this custard mixture as it cooks for 2 minutes. Remove from heat.

4 Use an electric mixer to beat egg whites until fluffy. Slowly beat in vanilla extract and sugar until combined and whites create stiff peaks.

5 Pour the custard mixture into the pre-baked pie crust. Spread the egg white meringue over top of custard.

6 Bake 11-13 minutes, or until meringue is golden brown. Let cool on counter for 3 hours before refrigerating until fully cooled.

Royal Riviera

Pears

Appetizers

Turkey, Gouda, and Pear Roll-Ups 79

Breakfast and Lunches

French Toast with Caramelized Pears 81
Spinach Salad with Gorgonzola and Pears 82
Sweet Potato and Pear Breakfast Hash 83
Grilled Ham and Pear Paninis 85
Pear and Pecan Coffee Cake 87
Wisconsin Cheddar Soup with Diced Pear 89

Main Courses and Sides

Sausage and Pear Stuffing 90
Matchstick Pear Slaw 91
Cranberry and Pear Stuffed Pork Loin 93
Sautéed Chicken with Walnuts and Pears 94

Desserts

Pear and Gingersnap Crisp 95
Pear and Custard Tart 97
Bread Pudding with Pears and Raisins 98
Pear and Mincemeat Pie 99
Sautéed Pears with Raspberry Sauce 101
Easy Pear Shortcakes 103

Turkey, Gouda, and Pear Roll-Ups

TOTAL PREPARATION TIME: 20 MINS   DIFFICULTY: EASY   SERVES: 4

Preparing these appetizers is an easy way to serve something light and distinctive at your next get-together. The combination of thick-sliced turkey, buttery cheese, peppery arugula leaves, and sweet pear is delicious in its simplicity.

Shopping List

8 thick slices deli turkey breast

4 slices smoked gouda cheese

1 pear, thinly sliced

1 cup fresh arugula leaves

1 Lay out all 8 slices of turkey breast on a large cutting board or sheet pan.

2 Slice the 4 slices of gouda cheese into thin strips.

3 Top each slice of turkey breast with a few strips of gouda cheese, a few slices of pear, and a few leaves of fresh arugula.

4 Roll each roll-up up and place seam-side down on a serving platter to keep closed. You can also secure with tooth-picks to help them hold together.

Cushman's Tips

This is also easily made with deli ham in place of the turkey and any buttery cheese in place of the gouda. Fontina, Havarti, and baby Swiss are all great cheese substitutions.

Royal Riviera
PEARS

French Toast with Caramelized Pears

TOTAL PREPARATION TIME: **40** MINS   DIFFICULTY: **EASY**   SERVES: **4**

This recipe for French toast is one of the best ways you can use a deliciously ripe pear. By caramelizing the pears in pure maple syrup there's no need to serve the French toast alongside any additional syrup.

Shopping List

CARAMELIZED PEARS

2 pears, cored and thinly sliced

1 teaspoon cornstarch

½ cup pure maple syrup

1 tablespoon butter

¼ teaspoon ground cinnamon

FRENCH TOAST

4 large eggs

1 cup milk

2 tablespoons light brown sugar

½ teaspoon vanilla extract

¼ teaspoon ground cinnamon

4 tablespoons butter or margarine

8 slices thick bread

1 Place sliced pears in a sauté pan over medium heat. Whisk cornstarch into maple syrup and add to sauté pan along with butter and cinnamon.

2 Sauté pears and sauce for 5-8 minutes, until sauce is thick and pears are tender. Remove from heat and set aside.

3 In a large mixing bowl, whisk together eggs, milk, brown sugar, vanilla extract, and cinnamon.

4 Place 1 tablespoon of butter in a large nonstick skillet over medium heat, heating until melted. Dip 2 slices of the thick bread into the egg and milk mixture and add to the pan, cooking 3-4 minutes on each side, until golden brown.

5 Repeat the last step 3 more times with the 3 remaining tablespoons of butter and 6 remaining slices of bread. Serve French toast smothered in the caramelized pears and maple syrup sauce.

Cushman's Tips

It should go without saying that you garnish this fruit smothered French toast with a nice big dollop of whipped cream!

Spinach Salad with Gorgonzola and Pears

TOTAL PREPARATION TIME: **20** MINS DIFFICULTY: EASY SERVES: **4**

I love to prepare this simple salad in two completely different ways. The first way is the way that the recipe is written: as a cold salad. The second way to prepare this is found in the tips: as a cold salad with warmed pears and pecans that you sprinkle over the gorgonzola cheese.

Shopping List

6 ounces fresh spinach leaves

1 pear, cored and diced

⅔ cup crumbled gorgonzola cheese

1 cup grape tomatoes

⅓ cup chopped pecans

RASPBERRY VINAIGRETTE

1 tablespoon balsamic vinegar

¼ cup fresh raspberries

1 teaspoon Dijon mustard

¼ teaspoon oregano

¼ teaspoon salt

⅛ teaspoon pepper

⅓ cup olive oil

1 Split the spinach equally between 4 bowls.

2 Top the spinach in each bowl with an equal amount of the remaining salad ingredients.

3 Create the dressing by adding balsamic vinegar, raspberries, Dijon mustard, oregano, salt, and pepper to a blender. Slowly add olive oil to the mixture as you blend to create a creamy vinaigrette.

4 Serve each salad drizzled with the vinaigrette.

Cushman's Tips

This is also very good when you sauté the pears and pecans for 2 minutes over medium heat and serve warm over top of the salad.

Sweet Potato and Pear Breakfast Hash

TOTAL PREPARATION TIME: 25 MINS   DIFFICULTY: EASY   SERVES: 6

While this is made from sweet potato, sweet pear, and sweet yellow onions, this is still a surprisingly savory breakfast alternative to traditional hash-browned potatoes. The bacon in this really brings it to another level, but when doesn't bacon do that?

Shopping List

4 cups cubed sweet potato, about ⅓ inch thick

2 tablespoons vegetable oil

2 slices bacon, chopped

1 yellow onion, diced

1 large pear, diced

1 teaspoon minced garlic

½ teaspoon paprika

¾ teaspoon salt

¼ teaspoon black pepper

1 Place cubed sweet potato in a large bowl of cold water and let sit 15 minutes. Drain well and pat dry with paper towels.

2 Heat vegetable oil and bacon in a large skillet over medium-high heat for 1 minute.

3 Add sweet potatoes to the skillet and sauté 5 minutes.

4 Add diced onion, pear, garlic, paprika, salt, and pepper to the skillet and continue sautéing until sweet potatoes are browned on the outside and tender on the inside and pears are tender, about 4-6 more minutes. Serve immediately.

Cushman's Tips

I like to serve an over-easy egg right over top of this hash, breaking the yolk into it before eating!

Royal Riviera
PEARS

Grilled Ham and Pear Paninis

TOTAL PREPARATION TIME: 20 MINS   **DIFFICULTY:** EASY   **SERVES:** 2

Paninis have become a new sandwich shop staple that few try to replicate at home. With any indoor grill, grill pan, or griddle, you can make a gourmet sandwich without waiting in lines or breaking the bank!

Shopping List

2 tablespoons mayonnaise

1 tablespoon whole-grain mustard

½ teaspoon honey

4 slices deli-style bread

4 slices Swiss cheese

½ pound sliced deli ham

½ cup fresh baby spinach leaves

1 pear, thinly sliced

nonstick cooking spray

1 In a small bowl, combine mayonnaise, mustard, and honey to create a honey-mustard sandwich spread.

2 Start preparing 2 separate sandwiches by spreading the sandwich spread on 2 slices of the bread. Top each with 1 slice of Swiss cheese.

3 Place an equal amount of the deli ham on each sandwich and then top with an equal amount of spinach leaves and pear slices.

4 Place another slice of Swiss cheese on each sandwich and top with the remaining slices of bread to finish.

5 Grill on an indoor grill, griddle, or Panini press sprayed with nonstick cooking spray until the bread is well toasted on both sides, or brown in a nonstick skillet over medium heat, about 4 minutes on each side.

Cushman's Tips

For a sandwich that is nice and hot throughout, you can pile up and pre-cook the ham in a skillet before assembling and grilling the sandwiches.

Royal Riviera
PEARS

Pear and Pecan Coffee Cake

TOTAL PREPARATION TIME: 1 HOUR   DIFFICULTY: HARD   SERVES: 12

Though this recipe is a little more time consuming than most others in this book, you'd be surprised by just how simple making a moist, homemade coffee cake can be.

Shopping List

nonstick cooking spray

1 stick butter, softened

1 cup sugar

2 large eggs

1 cup light sour cream

1 teaspoon vanilla extract

2 cups all-purpose flour

1 teaspoon baking soda

1 teaspoon baking powder

¼ teaspoon salt

¼ teaspoon cinnamon

2 pears, cored and thinly sliced

TOPPING

¾ cup light brown sugar

2 tablespoons butter or margarine

1 tablespoon all-purpose flour

1 teaspoon ground cinnamon

½ cup chopped pecans

1 Preheat oven to 350 degrees F. Spray a 9x13 baking dish with nonstick cooking spray.

2 Using an electric mixer, combine butter, sugar, eggs, sour cream, and vanilla extract.

3 In a separate bowl, combine the flour, baking soda, baking powder, salt, and cinnamon.

4 Using the electric mixer, slowly incorporate the dry mixture into the wet, until all is combined. Pour into the greased baking dish.

5 Top the cake batter in the baking dish with the thinly sliced pears, slightly overlapping them across the entire surface of the cake.

6 In a separate bowl, combine all Topping ingredients, until a dry and crumbly topping is created. Sprinkle topping evenly over the pears in the baking dish.

7 Bake 30-32 minutes, or until a toothpick inserted into the center of the cake comes out mostly clean. Let cool 10 minutes before slicing.

Royal Riviera
PEARS

Wisconsin Cheddar Soup with Diced Pear

TOTAL PREPARATION TIME: 25 MINS   DIFFICULTY: EASY   SERVES: 6

Topping a big bowl of warm Cheddar cheese soup with crisp and cold pear is a perfect combination that you just have to try to be able to understand! It's an interesting and delicious alternative to topping soup with crackers or croutons.

Shopping List

3 tablespoons butter or margarine

2 stalks celery, diced

3 green onions, sliced

1 cup shredded carrots

2 ½ cups chicken broth

1 cup beer

1 teaspoon Worcestershire sauce

⅛ teaspoon garlic powder

1 teaspoon sugar

¼ cup all-purpose flour

1 cup milk

2 cups shredded sharp Cheddar cheese

salt to taste

2 pears, peeled and diced

1 Place butter, celery, onions, and carrots in a stock pot over medium-high heat and cook 5 minutes, or until onions begin to brown.

2 Add chicken broth, beer, Worcestershire sauce, garlic powder, and sugar to the stock pot and stir to combine.

3 Bring up to a boil and let boil 10 minutes. Reduce heat to medium-low.

4 Whisk together the flour and milk and stir into the soup. Bring up to a simmer and let cook 3 minutes.

5 Stir in Cheddar cheese, just until all is melted and combined. Remove soup from heat, add salt to taste, and serve immediately, each bowl topped with a handful of fresh diced pear.

Cushman's Tips

You can use any beer, light or dark in color, in this soup. It adds a very nice flavor, but you can easily substitute an additional cup of chicken broth in its place, if you prefer.

Royal Riviera
PEARS

MAIN COURSES AND SIDES

Sausage and Pear Stuffing

TOTAL PREPARATION TIME: 1 HOUR   **DIFFICULTY: EASY**   **SERVES: 8**

This stuffing with pork sausage and diced pear makes a great side dish for roast turkey or chicken, but you don't need to think of it as strictly a holiday kind of thing! I even like to serve it underneath a simple baked chicken breast as a nice alternative to rice or potatoes.

Shopping List

nonstick cooking spray

1 pound ground pork sausage

1 yellow onion, diced

2 pears, peeled, cored, and diced

1 red bell pepper, diced

6 leaves fresh sage, chopped

1 (14-ounce) bag herbed stuffing cubes

2 cups chicken broth

⅔ cup apple juice

1 stick butter or margarine, melted

1 Preheat oven to 350 degrees F. Spray a 9x13 baking dish with nonstick cooking spray.

2 Add sausage to a large skillet over medium-high heat and cook 5 minutes, or until it is beginning to brown.

3 Add onion, pears, bell pepper, and sage, and continue to cook an additional 5 minutes, or until sausage is entirely browned and onion is translucent.

4 Stir stuffing cubes, chicken broth, and apple juice into the sausage mixture and then pour into the greased baking dish. Drizzle melted butter over top all.

5 Bake 40-45 minutes, or until stuffing is crunchy on top and soft in the middle. Serve immediately.

Cushman's Tips

The pork sausage that is best for this recipe is the kind that looks like ground beef and usually comes in pinched tubes in a refrigerated case.

Allen Cushman

Matchstick Pear Slaw

TOTAL PREPARATION TIME: **15** MINS   DIFFICULTY: **EASY**   SERVES: **8**

The crisp and sweet pears in this coleslaw bring a whole new flavor to the classic picnic salad. The trick to a beautiful slaw is cutting the pears into very thin and uniform "matchsticks."

Shopping List

¼ cup plain yogurt

2 tablespoons cider vinegar

2 teaspoons honey

½ teaspoon salt

¼ teaspoon pepper

¼ teaspoon onion powder

1 (12-ounce) bag shredded coleslaw mix

2 pears, julienned

1 In a large mixing bowl, combine yogurt, cider vinegar, honey, salt, pepper, and onion powder to create the slaw dressing.

2 Fold the shredded coleslaw mix and julienned pears into the slaw dressing, until all is well combined.

3 For best results: cover and refrigerate for 2 hours to let the flavors mingle before serving.

Cushman's Tips

*Y*ou can also make this into a more Asian style pear slaw by adding 6 chopped green onions, 1 tablespoon teriyaki sauce, and 2 teaspoons sesame oil.

Cranberry and Pear Stuffed Pork Loin

TOTAL PREPARATION TIME: 1 ½ HRS   DIFFICULTY: HARD   SERVES: 6

Fruit and pork are a perfect match, but few recipes can marry the two as well as this Cranberry and Pear Stuffed Pork Loin. This recipe is a great holiday alternative to baked hams or roast turkeys.

Shopping List

1 3-pound center-cut pork loin
1 tablespoon vegetable oil
¼ teaspoon dry thyme
¼ teaspoon garlic powder
¼ teaspoon salt
¼ teaspoon pepper
twine

STUFFING

1 cup herb-seasoned stuffing
⅓ cup apple juice
1 tablespoon butter, melted
⅓ cup sweetened dried cranberries
1 cup peeled and finely diced pear
2 teaspoons fresh chopped sage
¼ teaspoon salt

1 Preheat the oven to 325 degrees F. Butterfly pork loin by slicing down its entire length about ¾ of the way through. Lay the butterflied pork loin between two sheets of plastic wrap and pound with a meat mallet or rolling pin until flattened to about ⅓ inch thick.

2 Place pounded pork loin in a mixing bowl and cover with vegetable oil, thyme, garlic powder, salt, and pepper. Toss until pork is well coated.

3 In another mixing bowl, combine all Stuffing ingredients.

4 Lay out 4 lengths of twine and place the pounded and seasoned pork loin over top of them. Spoon the stuffing over the entire surface of the pork loin and then roll up into a pinwheel. Pull each of the 4 pieces of twine over the top of the rolled roast and tie to secure.

5 Transfer tied roast to a sheet pan and bake 60-70 minutes, or until internal temperature reaches 145 degrees F. Remove from oven and let rest at least 5 minutes before removing twine and slicing.

Cushman's Tips

You can also use two pork tenderloins (about 1 ¼ pound each) in place of the center-cut pork loin. You can pound the tenderloins and then simply overlap them to roll into one large roast.

Sautéed Chicken with Walnuts and Pears

TOTAL PREPARATION TIME: 20 MINS   **DIFFICULTY: EASY**   **SERVES: 4**

This sweet and savory entrée is like an American version of Chinese sweet and sour chicken. Cubed chicken is sautéed in a buttery sauce with julienned pears and crunchy walnut halves. I love to serve it over rice pilaf, but it goes great with any potato side dish as well.

Shopping List

1 ½ pounds boneless, skinless chicken breasts, cut into cubes

2 tablespoons vegetable oil

⅛ teaspoon salt

⅛ teaspoon pepper

3 tablespoons butter or margarine

2 pears, thinly julienned

1 tablespoon flour

⅔ cup apple juice

2 tablespoons soy sauce

1 teaspoon sugar

1 teaspoon minced garlic

⅔ cup walnut halves

1 Place cubed chicken and vegetable oil in a skillet over medium-high heat and season with the salt and pepper. Cook 4 minutes, just until chicken begins to brown.

2 Add butter and pears to the skillet and continue to sauté for 2 minutes.

3 Whisk together flour, apple juice, soy sauce, sugar, and minced garlic and pour into the skillet. Cook for 2 minutes, or until thick.

4 Stir walnut halves into the skillet and sauté 1 final minute, or until chicken is cooked throughout. Serve immediately.

Cushman's Tips

You can also make this without cutting the chicken breasts into cubes for a nicer presentation, but you will need to start with relatively thin chicken breasts and sauté for 5 minutes on each side in step 1.

Pear and Gingersnap Crisp

TOTAL PREPARATION TIME: 1 HOUR   DIFFICULTY: EASY   SERVES: 6

Gingersnaps have always been a favorite of mine, but it was only recently that I had the idea of making this gingersnap topped pear crisp. Ginger goes really great with fruit, especially the pears in this, but rather than take my word for it, why don't you SNAP to it?

Shopping List

nonstick cooking spray

6 cups peeled and sliced pears

2 teaspoons lemon juice

½ cup sugar

1 tablespoon cornstarch

1 teaspoon ground cinnamon

¼ teaspoon ground ginger

TOPPING

1 cup gingersnap cookies

¼ cup light brown sugar

3 tablespoons butter, cold

1 Preheat oven to 375 degrees F. Spray an 8x8 baking dish with nonstick cooking spray.

2 In a large mixing bowl, combine pears, lemon juice, sugar, cornstarch, cinnamon, and ground ginger, and pour into the greased baking dish.

3 In a food processor, combine all Topping ingredients and pulse just until cookies are crumbled and butter is chopped and dispersed throughout.

4 Drop Topping by the large spoonful over top of the fruit mixture in the baking dish.

5 Bake for 40-45 minutes, or until bubbly hot and topping is crisp. Let cool for at least 5 minutes before spooning into serving bowls.

Cushman's Tips

Make this into a Vanilla Pear Crisp by omitting the ground ginger and adding 1 teaspoon of vanilla extract to the fruit mixture. Next, substitute vanilla wafer cookies in place of the gingersnaps to make the topping.

Pear and Custard Tart

TOTAL PREPARATION TIME: 1 HOUR   DIFFICULTY: HARD   SERVES: 8-12

This giant custard-filled tart is an absolute beauty! While it looks best when baked in an 11-inch fluted tart pan, you can also bake it in any 10-inch pie plate if that is more convenient for you.

Shopping List

1 9-inch refrigerated pie crust, thawed

FILLING

5 large eggs

1 ¼ cups sugar

½ cup milk

¼ cup all-purpose flour

1 teaspoon vanilla extract

PEARS

2 pears, peeled, cored, and thinly sliced

2 tablespoons pure maple syrup

¼ teaspoon ground cinnamon

1 Preheat oven to 400 degrees F. Use a rolling pin to roll out pie crust, fitting it to an 11-inch tart pan. Fill crust in tart pan with pie weights or poke air holes to vent, and bake 7 minutes, just until lightly cooked. Carefully remove weights.

2 Reduce oven temperature to 350 degrees F. In a mixing bowl, whisk together all Filling ingredients and pour into the pre-baked crust.

3 In another mixing bowl, toss the pears in maple syrup and cinnamon until fully coated. Carefully arrange slices, slightly overlapping, over the entire surface of the tart.

4 Bake 35-40 minutes, or until the pears and crust have browned and the custard filling is set.

5 Let cool on counter for 2 hours before refrigerating at least 1 additional hour. Slice into 8-12 slices and serve chilled.

Cushman's Tips

*U*sing pie weights or poking air holes in the crust will ensure that air bubbles do not ruin the shape of the crust as it pre-bakes. If you use the air hole method, be sure to sprinkle the bottom of the crust with a teaspoon of flour before filling with the custard filling to ensure that the custard does not seep out of the air holes.

Bread Pudding with Pears and Raisins

TOTAL PREPARATION TIME: 1 HOUR   DIFFICULTY: MEDIUM   SERVES: 8

Bread pudding is a wonderful dessert for family dinners and gatherings as you can prepare everything in advance and refrigerate until ready to bake. It only gets better as it sits and the custard permeates the bread.

Shopping List

nonstick cooking spray

4 cups cubed bread

2 cups peeled, cored, and thinly sliced pears

⅓ cup golden raisins

1 ⅔ cups milk

3 tablespoons butter or margarine, melted

2 large eggs

1 cup light brown sugar

½ teaspoon vanilla extract

1 teaspoon ground cinnamon

SAUCE

1 stick butter

1 cup light brown sugar

½ teaspoon vanilla extract

¼ teaspoon salt

1 Preheat oven to 350 degrees F. Spray a 3 quart baking dish with nonstick cooking spray.

2 Toss together bread, pears, and raisins and pour into baking dish.

3 In a mixing bowl, whisk together all remaining ingredients and pour over bread mixture in baking dish. Cover and refrigerate for at least 30 minutes.

4 Uncover and bake 45-50 minutes, or until center of pudding is set and top is beginning to brown.

5 In a sauce pan over medium-high heat, combine all Sauce ingredients and bring up to a simmer. Let simmer 1 minute before serving drizzled over bowls of the finished bread pudding.

Cushman's Tips

To make the sauce into a more traditional rum sauce, simply substitute 2 tablespoons of rum in place of the vanilla extract. Simmer for 2 additional minutes to ensure that the alcohol is fully cooked out.

Pear and Mincemeat Pie

TOTAL PREPARATION TIME: 1 HOUR   DIFFICULTY: MEDIUM   SERVES: 8

Mincemeat has been a very mysterious thing to many people, but it is really just a mixture of chopped apples and raisins or dates. I find it to be incredibly delicious, especially in this pie with a top crust made of sliced pears.

Shopping List

1 9-inch refrigerated pie crust, thawed

1 tablespoon all-purpose flour

1 (18-ounce) jar mincemeat

2 small pears, peeled, cored, and thinly sliced

¼ cup all-purpose flour

¼ cup light brown sugar

2 tablespoons butter, cold

½ teaspoon ground cinnamon

1 Preheat oven to 425 degrees F. Press pie crust into the bottom of a 9-inch pie plate.

2 Sprinkle the inside of the pie crust with 1 tablespoon of flour and then fill with the mincemeat.

3 Carefully arrange pear slices, overlapping, over the entire surface of the pie.

4 Place all remaining ingredients in a food processor and pulse just a few times to create a topping. Topping should be dry and crumbly.

5 Spoon topping evenly over the surface of the pears.

6 Bake 40-45 minutes, or until the topping and crust have browned.

Cushman's Tips

If the crust is over-browning before the topping is crisp, simply create a ring of aluminum foil and cover the edges of the crust for the remainder of the baking.

Sautéed Pears with Raspberry Sauce

TOTAL PREPARATION TIME: **20** MINS   DIFFICULTY: **EASY**   SERVES: **4**

This is one of my favorite pear dessert recipes for three reasons: 1. It's a truly elegant dessert to serve to dinner guests. 2. It's a perfectly portioned dessert that isn't too heavy after a large meal. 3. It's deceptively quick and easy to prepare!

Shopping List

2 pears, peeled, cored, and cut in half

1 tablespoon honey

¼ cup sugar

⅓ cup apple juice

1 cup fresh raspberries

1 Brush pears with honey and place facedown in a sauté pan over medium heat.

2 Let cook 5-6 minutes, or until lightly browned.

3 Flip pears and add sugar, apple juice, and raspberries. Cover and let simmer together for 8-10 minutes, or until pears are tender.

4 Remove pears and set aside. Use a potato masher or heavy spoon to mash the raspberries into a sauce.

5 Serve each pear half smothered with the warm raspberry sauce.

Cushman's Tips

You can also make this with wedges of pears, rather than halves. When using wedges, you should reduce the cooking time in step 3 to only 3-5 minutes, depending on how thick you cut the wedges.

Easy Pear Shortcakes

TOTAL PREPARATION TIME: **1** HOUR   DIFFICULTY: EASY   SERVES: **8**

Although shortcakes are typically smothered in sweet strawberry sauce, I hope to change that with this recipe for a delicious pear version that is absolutely brimming with fresh pear flavor!

Shopping List

1 (18.25-ounce) box yellow cake mix

3 large eggs

1 cup water

⅓ cup vegetable oil

8 ounces light sour cream

¼ teaspoon salt

3 teaspoons cornstarch

1 ¼ cups apple juice

3 pears, peeled and sliced

½ cup sugar

whipped cream

1 Preheat oven to 350 degrees F. In an electric mixer, combine yellow cake mix, eggs, water, vegetable oil, sour cream, and salt. Beat until smooth and creamy, about 2 minutes.

2 Pour cake batter into a 5x9 loaf pan, about ¾ of the way full. Discard any leftover batter.

3 Bake 45-50 minutes, or until the top is puffy and browned and a toothpick in-

serted into the center comes out mostly clean. Let cool completely.

4 Meanwhile, whisk cornstarch into the apple juice and combine with the pears and sugar in a sauté pan over medium-high heat. Bring up to a simmer and cook 4-5 minutes, until sauce is thick and pears are tender. Transfer to the refrigerator to cool.

5 Create the pear shortcakes by slicing the loaf of cake into 8 thick slices. Slice each slice in half. Place a ½ slice of cake at the bottom of a dish and top with a large spoonful of the chilled pears and sauce. Top with another ½ slice of cake and then garnish with whipped cream to finish.

Cushman's Tips

*F*or something even simpler, you can also make these with store-bought shortcake cups in place of the sliced yellow cake.

Golden Pineapples

Appetizers and Snacks

Breakfast and Lunches

Main Courses

Desserts

Pineapple Salsa

TOTAL PREPARATION TIME: 15 MINS   **DIFFICULTY: EASY**   **SERVES: 8**

This sweet and savory salsa may seem like it would be too sweet for your average tortilla chip dipping, but I promise you that it is not! With a hint of spice from diced jalapeño and red onion and the classic Mexican flavors of lime juice and cilantro, this salsa has all the traditional flavors you love, but the pineapple adds something new without being overbearing.

Shopping List

1 ½ cups finely diced pineapple

1 (15-ounce) can black beans, drained

½ cup diced red bell pepper

1 jalapeño, seeded and diced

½ cup diced red onion

¼ cup fresh chopped cilantro

juice of 1 lime

¼ teaspoon salt

1 In a large mixing bowl, combine all ingredients, tossing well.

2 For best results, cover and refrigerate for 2 hours to let the flavors mingle before serving. Serve alongside tortilla chips or as a topping on tacos, fajitas, or burritos.

Cushman's Tips

"Seasoned recipe" canned black beans work very well in this recipe; just be sure to thoroughly drain or the final salsa may be too salty.

For mild salsa, be sure to thoroughly remove the jalapeño seeds before chopping as that's where most of their heat comes from.

Sweet and Sour Chicken Kabobs

TOTAL PREPARATION TIME: 20 MINS   DIFFICULTY: EASY   SERVES: 4

These sweet and savory chicken kabobs are a great Asian alternative to barbecue chicken. Serving on skewers allows you to grill the chicken right alongside chunks of fresh pineapple and green bell pepper, locking in all kinds of great flavors.

Shopping List

1 pound chicken breasts, cut into 1-inch cubes

2 tablespoons ketchup

2 tablespoons low-sodium soy sauce

1 tablespoon white vinegar

1 tablespoon vegetable oil

1 tablespoon light brown sugar

2 teaspoons minced garlic

⅛ teaspoon ground ginger

2 cups cut pineapple chunks

1 large red bell pepper, chopped

metal or bamboo skewers, soaked in water

1 Add chicken breast cubes, ketchup, soy sauce, white vinegar, vegetable oil, brown sugar, garlic, and ground ginger to a container or food storage bag and toss all to combine. Refrigerate for 1 hour to marinate.

2 Preheat a grill, indoor grill, or grill pan to medium-high.

3 Remove chicken from marinade and thread onto skewers with the pineapple chunks and chopped red bell pepper, alternating between the three as you fill the skewer.

4 Place all skewers on a sheet pan and pour remaining marinade over top all for one final coat.

5 Remove skewers from sheet pan and place on grill. Grill 10-12 minutes, flipping halfway through. Cut into the thickest chunk of chicken to test for doneness before serving. Makes about 8 full skewers.

Cushman's Tips

It is extremely important that bamboo skewers be soaked in water for at least 30 minutes before grilling; otherwise, they may catch on fire.

Pineapple Cream Cheese Spread

TOTAL PREPARATION TIME: **10** MINS   DIFFICULTY: EASY   SERVES: **8**

This Pineapple Cream Cheese Spread is a perfect change of pace for the morning routine. Spread this on bagels or crispy toast, or use just about anywhere you'd use regular cream cheese. This is also a good dip to serve alongside hearty crackers or celery sticks.

Shopping List

8 ounces cream cheese, softened

1 cup roughly chopped pineapple, room temperature

1 tablespoon light brown sugar

⅛ teaspoon salt

1 Place all ingredients in the bowl of a food processor.

2 Pulse just until pineapple is finely chopped and dispersed throughout the cream cheese.

3 Refrigerate for 30 minutes, or until cheese has thickened. Serve chilled.

Cushman's Tips

You can soften the cream cheese easily by heating 1-2 minutes using the microwave's defrost setting. Just be sure to remove the cheese from its metal wrapping first!

Tropical Fruit Salad with Toasted Coconut

TOTAL PREPARATION TIME: 15 MINS   DIFFICULTY: EASY   SERVES: 8

This tropical fruit salad includes pineapples, oranges, and mangos tossed with lime zest and crunchy toasted coconut. The nutty taste of the toasted coconut and a splash of creamy coconut milk really help offset the acidity of the tropical fruit.

Shopping List

2 cups pineapple chunks

2 large oranges or HoneyBells, peeled, seeded, and segmented

2 mangos, peeled and chopped

zest of 1 small lime

2 tablespoons coconut milk

1 tablespoon honey

½ cup sweetened coconut flakes

1 Preheat oven to 350 degrees F.

2 Place pineapple chunks, orange segments, chopped mango, lime zest, coconut milk, and honey in a large bowl.

3 Meanwhile, spread the sweetened coconut flakes across a sheet pan and bake 5-7 minutes, just until they turn a light shade of brown.

4 Add the toasted coconut to the bowl of fruit and toss all to combine. Serve chilled.

Cushman's Tips

This is best with the crunchy and aromatic toasted coconut but can also be made easier with just untoasted coconut flakes.

Chicken and Pineapple Lo Mein

TOTAL PREPARATION TIME: **25** MINS   DIFFICULTY: **EASY**   SERVES: **4**

Lo Mein is a great Chinese noodle dish that is easily recreated at home. I use linguine pasta as it's nice and thick, which keeps it from overcooking when stir fried along with the other ingredients.

Shopping List

12 ounces dry linguine pasta

1 tablespoon sesame oil

1 pound boneless, skinless chicken breasts, chopped

salt and pepper

4 tablespoons butter or margarine

3 tablespoons soy sauce

2 teaspoons minced garlic

1 cup fresh chopped pineapple

1 cup frozen peas and carrot mix

4 green onions, sliced

1 Prepare linguine by boiling for 3 minutes less than the package directions. Drain and rinse under cold water.

2 Meanwhile, place sesame oil in a very large skillet or wok over medium-high heat. Add the chopped chicken and season lightly with salt and pepper. Sauté until chicken is browned, about 7 minutes.

3 Add all remaining ingredients to the skillet and stir until butter has melted.

4 Add the rinsed linguine to the skillet and continue to stir fry for 3 more minutes, or until chicken is cooked throughout. Serve immediately.

Cushman's Tips

*Y*ou can use any frozen bagged stir fry vegetables in place of the pea and carrot mix.

Golden
PINEAPPLES

Hawaiian Pizza

TOTAL PREPARATION TIME: 2 HRS   **DIFFICULTY: MEDIUM**   **SERVES: 4**

Putting chunks of pineapple on a pizza used to be a pretty off-the-wall concept, but Hawaiian pizzas are now quite the popular pie! This recipe makes a Hawaiian pizza with fresh pineapple chunks, which is something you definitely can't get with delivery.

Shopping List

1 (.25-ounce) envelope active dry yeast

1 teaspoon sugar

1 cup warm water

2 ½ cups flour

¾ teaspoon salt

nonstick cooking spray

1 tablespoon cornmeal

¾ cup pizza sauce

1 ½ cups shredded mozzarella cheese

5 slices Canadian bacon, quartered

1 cup pineapple chunks, patted dry

1 (2.25-ounce) can sliced black olives, drained

1 Stir yeast and sugar into the warm water and let sit 15 minutes.

2 In a large mixing bowl, add yeast mixture to the flour and salt. Knead with your hands until a ball of dough is formed. Place ball of dough in a large bowl sprayed with nonstick cooking spray. Cover with plastic wrap and let sit in a warm place to rise for 1 hour, or until doubled.

3 On a well-floured surface, roll dough into a circular shape with a rolling pin, until about ¼ inch thin. Let sit 15 minutes to rise again.

4 Preheat oven to 450 degrees F. Spray a large baking sheet with nonstick cooking spray and then sprinkle with cornmeal.

5 Crust will have retracted; pull it in all directions until it is ¼ inch thin again. Transfer to the cornmeal dusted baking sheet. Spread pizza sauce over crust and then top with the mozzarella cheese, Canadian bacon, pineapple chunks, and black olives. Do not apply too much pressure to the crust once on baking sheet or it may stick!

6 Bake 15-20 minutes, or until cheese is bubbly and crust is starting to brown.

Cushman's Tips

The shape of your pizza is definitely not as important as the taste, so feel free to make it oval or rectangular, especially if you are working with a smaller baking sheet!

Glazed Ham Steaks with Pineapple Rings

TOTAL PREPARATION TIME: **20** MINS   DIFFICULTY: EASY   SERVES: **4**

I love ham steaks, as you can get all the goodness of baking a ham without all of the baking time. And while I do love leftovers, sometimes a whole ham can be a little overwhelming leftovers-wise. This recipe tops ham steaks with a mustard glaze, then fresh pineapple rings, and then another glaze of brown sugar!

Shopping List

2 large ham steaks

2 tablespoons butter or margarine, melted

3 tablespoons coarse or Dijon mustard

4-8 pineapple rings

¼ cup light brown sugar

1 Preheat oven to 350 degrees F. Place ham steaks on an aluminum foil-lined sheet pan.

2 In a small bowl, combine butter and mustard and then spread over both ham steaks.

3 Bake until steaks are warmed throughout, about 10 minutes.

4 Top each steak with 2-4 pineapple slices (covering the entire surface of the steaks). Sprinkle brown sugar over top all.

5 Switch oven to broil and broil the pineapple-topped steaks until the sugar begins to brown, about 3-4 minutes. Serve immediately.

Cushman's Tips

*I*f you'd prefer to skip the broiling step, you can simply top these with the pineapple and sugar from the beginning and bake 15-20 minutes at 350 degrees F. It may not brown as well, but it should still come out pretty good.

Hawaiian Burgers

TOTAL PREPARATION TIME: 30 MINS   **DIFFICULTY: EASY**   **SERVES: 4**

I love grilled pineapple, especially on these Hawaiian Burgers. Served topped with not only grilled pineapple but also strips of bacon and a Teriyaki Mayo, these burgers are a sweet and savory taste of the tropics!

Shopping List

1 pound lean ground beef

2 tablespoons teriyaki sauce

¼ teaspoon pepper

⅛ teaspoon garlic powder

4 thick pineapple rings

8 strips cooked bacon

buns and fixings

TERIYAKI MAYO

½ cup mayonnaise

1 tablespoon teriyaki sauce

1 teaspoon minced garlic

1 In a mixing bowl, combine ground beef, teriyaki sauce, pepper, and garlic powder.

2 Form ground beef mixture into 4 large burger patties.

3 Preheat a grill, an indoor grill, or a grill pan to high. Grill burgers for 5-7 minutes on each side, or until your desired doneness.

4 Place pineapple rings on grill, grilling just long enough to create grill marks.

5 In a mixing bowl, combine all Teriyaki Mayo ingredients

6 Serve burgers on buns, each topped with 2 slices bacon and 1 grilled pineapple ring. Serve topped with your favorite fixings and smothered with the Teriyaki mayo.

Cushman's Tips

For the best burgers, butter and throw the buns on the grill just long enough to mark before assembling.

Pineapple and Pistachio Delight

TOTAL PREPARATION TIME: **15** MINS   DIFFICULTY: EASY   SERVES: **8**

This is one of those classic parfait recipes that everyone has their own take on. Usually made with chopped pecans, I like to make my version with chopped pistachios as it really highlights the pistachio pudding swirled throughout.

Shopping List

1 (3.3 ounce) box pistachio instant pudding mix

¼ cup milk

1 ½ cups finely minced pineapple

¾ cup chopped pistachios

1 (12-ounce) tub non-dairy whipped topping, thawed

1 In a large bowl, combine pudding mix, milk, minced pineapple, and pistachios.

2 Gently fold in non-dairy whipped topping until all is well combined. Cover and chill for at least 30 minutes before serving.

Cushman's Tips

You should measure the minced pineapple after mincing it and not before, because otherwise you won't be getting as much of the pineapple goodness you should be!

Pineapple Upside-Down Cake

TOTAL PREPARATION TIME: **1 ½ HRS**   DIFFICULTY: **MEDIUM**   SERVES: **12**

You simply cannot have an entire chapter of pineapple recipes without the quintessential Pineapple Upside-Down Cake. I make mine in a big round cake pan to maximize the surface area. More surface area means more fresh pineapple on the top to go around!

Shopping List

nonstick cooking spray

PINEAPPLE TOPPING

4 tablespoons butter or margarine, melted

½ cup light brown sugar

½ teaspoon rum extract

5-7 fresh pineapple slices

7-10 maraschino or fresh pitted cherries

CAKE

1 (18.25-ounce) box yellow cake mix

1 cup pineapple juice

⅓ cup water

⅓ cup vegetable oil

3 large eggs

½ cup sweetened coconut flakes

1 Preheat oven to 350 degrees F. Spray a 9 or 10-inch cake pan with nonstick cooking spray. Important: You must use a cake pan with a depth of at least 2 inches.

2 Whisk together melted butter, brown sugar, and rum extract, and pour into the greased cake pan.

3 Arrange the pineapple slices over top of the brown sugar mixture in the pan. You may need to cut them to cover as much of the surface with pineapple as you can. Fill in the center of the pineapple rings and any other spaces with cherries.

4 In an electric mixer, combine all Cake ingredients, except coconut. Beat until smooth and creamy, about 2 minutes. Fold coconut into the batter.

5 Pour cake batter over the Pineapple Topping in the cake pan. Important: If using the smaller, 9-inch, pan, you should only fill the pan ¾ of the way full and then discard any remaining batter.

6 Bake 45-55 minutes, or until the top is puffy and browned and a toothpick inserted into the center comes out mostly clean. Let cool completely before inverting onto a serving platter to present upside-down.

Cushman's Tips

You can also make this with a splash of real rum in place of the rum extract for a more classic preparation.

Grilled Pineapple S'mores

TOTAL PREPARATION TIME: 30 MINS   DIFFICULTY: EASY   SERVES: 4

These Grilled Pineapple S'mores are a huge hit with kids. The smokiness of the grilled pineapple really helps make up for the fact that the marshmallows are heated in the microwave and not over a campfire! Each batch makes 4 large s'mores.

Shopping List

4 whole graham cracker sheets

4 rings pineapple

¼ cup semisweet chocolate chips

½ cup miniature marshmallows

1 Break the whole graham cracker sheets in half to create 8 graham cracker squares.

2 Preheat a grill, indoor grill, or grill pan to high.

3 Grill pineapple for 1-2 minutes on each side, just until marked by the grill.

4 Cut each grilled pineapple ring into large chunks and place an equal amount on 4 of the graham cracker squares. Reserve the other 4 cracker squares to top the s'mores later.

5 Top the pineapple on each cracker square with an equal amount of the chocolate chips and miniature marshmallows.

6 Microwave on high for 30-45 seconds, just until chocolate and marshmallows begin to melt.

7 Top each s'more with the remaining cracker squares and serve immediately.

Cushman's Tips

*T*he whole graham cracker sheets this recipe calls for are referring to 4 of the long rectangular cracker sheets that have 4 smaller crackers on each.

Pineapple and Macadamia Bars

TOTAL PREPARATION TIME: **50** MINS   DIFFICULTY: **MEDIUM**   SERVES: **10**

These Pineapple and Macadamia Bars have a pastry crust and a creamy custard and crushed pineapple filling with chopped macadamia nuts. Because the goodness just couldn't stop there, I like to top these with shredded coconut for the perfect tropical garnish.

Shopping List

1 cup all-purpose flour

¼ cup light brown sugar

1 stick butter, cold

1 pinch salt

FILLING

3 large eggs

1 cup sugar

3 tablespoons all-purpose flour

¼ teaspoon baking powder

1 cup minced pineapple

½ cup macadamia nuts, roughly chopped

sweetened coconut flakes, for garnish

1 Preheat oven to 350 degrees F. Line an 8x8 inch baking dish with parchment paper.

2 In a mixing bowl, mash together flour, light brown sugar, cold butter, and salt to create the crust. Press into the bottom of the paper-lined baking dish and bake 15 minutes.

3 In a clean mixing bowl, whisk together eggs, sugar, flour, and baking powder. Fold in pineapple and macadamia nuts and pour over the pre-baked crust.

4 Bake for 25-30 minutes, or until the custard filling is set.

5 Let cool on counter for 2 hours before refrigerating at least 1 additional hour. Slice in half horizontally and then into 5 sections vertically to make 10 bars. Serve chilled, topped with a sprinkling of coconut flakes, for garnish.

Cushman's Tips

You can also use pecans in place of the macadamia nuts if you would prefer.

Oregold Peaches

Appetizers, Snacks, and Beverages

Chicken Quesadillas with Jalapeño Peach Salsa 125
Orange Peach Sangria 126
Spiced Peach Milkshakes 127
Sweet Pickled Peaches 129
Grilled Peach Skewers with Gorgonzola 130
Mango Peach Smoothies 131

Breakfast and Lunches

Honey Peach Muffins 133
Peach Turnovers 135
Southwestern Chicken Salad with Peaches 136
Peachy French Toast Casserole 137
Pork Tenderloin and Peach Salad 139
Peach Bottom Pancakes 140

Main Courses

Slow Cooker Peach Pork Chops 141
Grilled Peach Chicken 143
Ginger Peach Chicken Breasts 144
Barbecue Peach Glazed Salmon 145

Desserts

Peach Ice Cream 147
Poached Peaches with Yogurt 148
Peach Sorbet 149
Maple Peach Cobbler 151

Chicken Quesadillas with Jalapeño Peach Salsa

TOTAL PREPARATION TIME: 30 MINS   DIFFICULTY: EASY   SERVES: 4

Quesadillas make a great and simple lunch, especially when paired with a fresh salsa like the one in this recipe. The jalapeño in the salsa adds a little bit of heat, but it's nothing that serving alongside a dollop of sour cream can't cool down!

Shopping List

SALSA

1 large tomato, chopped

1 peach, pitted and chopped

½ jalapeño, seeded and chopped

¼ cup diced onion

1 tablespoon fresh chopped cilantro

1 tablespoon white vinegar

1 teaspoon honey

QUESADILLAS

4 tablespoons butter or margarine

4 flour tortillas

2 cups shredded Mexican cheese blend

10 ounces cooked chicken

1 In a mixing bowl, toss together all Salsa ingredients to create the Jalapeño Peach Salsa. Refrigerate until ready to serve.

2 Place 1 tablespoon of the butter in a large nonstick skillet over medium heat, heating until melted.

3 Place 1 flour tortilla in the hot pan and sprinkle ¼ of the cheese and chicken over its entire surface.

4 Once the cheese is beginning to melt, use a spatula to fold the tortilla over onto itself, creating a sealed half-moon shape. Continue cooking until both sides are golden brown.

5 Repeat steps 2-4 to create the remaining 3 quesadillas. Serve each alongside a generous scoop of the Jalapeño Peach Salsa.

Cushman's Tips

The precooked chicken breast strips sold in the refrigerated case of your grocery store work perfectly in this recipe, especially the Southwestern seasoned ones!

Oregold
PEACHES

Orange Peach Sangria

TOTAL PREPARATION TIME: 15 MINS   **DIFFICULTY: EASY**   **SERVES: 8**

This fruity red wine punch is served with actual wedges of peach and slices of orange floating right in it. This makes a giant pitcher's worth, so be sure that you have a few friends to enjoy it with!

Shopping List

1 bottle dry red wine

1 ½ cups peach nectar

1 ½ cups orange juice

2 cups lemon-lime soda

2 cups sliced peaches

1 small orange, thinly sliced (with peel)

2 cups ice

1 Chill all ingredients before starting.

2 In a large pitcher or punch bowl, combine all ingredients, stirring well.

3 Stir in ice just before serving.

Cushman's Tips

Peach nectar is usually sold in cartons in either the juice aisle or the Latin food aisle. White grape juice can be substituted for an equally delicious drink, but much of the peachy flavor will be lost.

Spiced Peach Milkshakes

TOTAL PREPARATION TIME: 15 MINS   **DIFFICULTY: EASY**   **SERVES: 2**

Now that it is getting harder to find milkshakes that are actually made from real ice cream and real milk, it's easier to simply make them yourself at home! These milkshakes are extra thick and flavored with fresh peach and a touch of spice.

Shopping List

1 large peach, cut into wedges

2 large scoops vanilla ice cream

1 ½ cups milk

½ teaspoon vanilla extract

1 tablespoon sugar

¼ teaspoon apple pie spice

whipped cream, for garnish

1 Place peach wedges in a single layer on a dish or platter. Freeze for at least 2 hours, until frozen solid.

2 Place frozen peach wedges, ice cream, milk, vanilla extract, sugar, and apple pie spice into a blender.

3 Blend until milkshake is entirely smooth, about 2 minutes. Serve garnished with whipped cream.

Cushman's Tips

For regular peach milkshakes, simply omit the apple pie spice.

If you do not have any apple pie spice on hand, you can substitute ¼ teaspoon ground cinnamon and a very small pinch of ground nutmeg.

Sweet Pickled Peaches

TOTAL PREPARATION TIME: 1 HOUR   DIFFICULTY: MEDIUM   SERVES: 16

I am pretty sure that pickled peaches are only a southern kind of thing, but I've got to say that that is a real shame! Though they are best after at least a few days of marinating, these spiced peaches are in a brine that most resembles the one used to make bread and butter pickles.

Shopping List

8 peaches, peeled and cut into wedges

cinnamon sticks

whole cloves

¾ cup white vinegar

¾ cup water

3 cups sugar

1 Place peach wedges into heavy glass jars, filling about ¾ of the way full. Add 1 whole cinnamon stick and sprinkle a teaspoon of whole cloves into each jar of peaches.

2 Place vinegar, water, and sugar into a stock pot and heat over medium-high.

3 Bring sugar mixture up to a boil and let boil 7 minutes. Remove from heat and let cool 15 minutes.

4 Pour the cooked sugar mixture into each jar of peaches, filling to about ¾ of an inch from the top.

5 Close jars and refrigerate for 5 days before serving.

Cushman's Tips

You can also seal and sterilize actual pickling jars by processing in a water bath for 10 minutes. This way you can have peaches all year long!

Grilled Peach Skewers with Gorgonzola

TOTAL PREPARATION TIME: 30 MINS   DIFFICULTY: EASY   SERVES: 6

Grilled peaches, honey, and gorgonzola cheese make the perfect sweet and savory combination in these great party skewers. Makes 18 bite-sized skewers, so there will definitely be enough to go around.

Shopping List

short bamboo skewers

3 peaches, each cut into 6 wedges

6 ounces crumbled gorgonzola cheese

¼ cup honey

1 Soak 18 short bamboo skewers in water for 30 minutes. Preheat a grill, indoor grill, or grill pan to high.

2 Skewer 1 wedge of peach onto the end of each bamboo skewer.

3 Grill skewers for about 1 minute on each side, just long enough to warm the peach and create grill marks.

4 Place skewers on a large serving platter and sprinkle the gorgonzola cheese over top all.

5 Drizzle skewers with honey and serve.

Cushman's Tips

These should be picked up carefully and served with plates as the gorgonzola cheese can easily fall off of the peaches.

Mango Peach Smoothies

TOTAL PREPARATION TIME: 15 MINS   **DIFFICULTY:** EASY   **SERVES:** 4

Mangos are one of my favorites of the fruits that did not get their own category in this book! (Something for a second book?) In this recipe, I've combined mango with peaches and milk to make a smoothie that is nearly as thick and delicious as ice cream.

Shopping List

2 large peaches, peeled, cored, and cut into wedges

¾ cup chopped mango

2 cups milk

3 tablespoons sugar

⅛ teaspoon vanilla extract

1 Place peach wedges and chopped mango in a single layer on a dish or platter. Freeze for at least 2 hours, until frozen solid.

2 Place frozen peach wedges, mango, and all remaining ingredients into a blender.

3 Blend until drink is entirely smooth, about 2 minutes. Serve immediately.

Cushman's Tips

This recipe is a great way to use up peaches and mangos that are a little over-ripe. Though they may have soft spots, these over-ripe fruits are very concentrated with flavor.

Oregold
PEACHES

Honey Peach Muffins

TOTAL PREPARATION TIME: 35 MINS   DIFFICULTY: MEDIUM   SERVES: 12

These golden muffins are sweet and delicious, with just the right amount of fresh peach flavor. I even use puréed peaches in the batter to keep the butter down to only 2 tablespoons, which is a lot less than you would normally find in a muffin recipe.

Shopping List

DRY INGREDIENTS

1 ½ cups all-purpose flour

½ cup sugar

⅓ cup light brown sugar

1 ½ teaspoons baking powder

½ teaspoon ground cinnamon

¼ teaspoon salt

WET INGREDIENTS

1 large egg, beaten

½ cup puréed peaches

½ cup milk

2 tablespoons butter or margarine, melted

2 tablespoons honey

1 cup peeled and chopped peaches

1 Preheat oven to 375 degrees F. In a large mixing bowl, combine all Dry Ingredients, tossing well.

2 In a separate mixing bowl, combine all Wet Ingredients, except the chopped peaches.

3 Pour the Wet Ingredients into the Dry Ingredients, stirring all to combine into a batter. Gently fold chopped peaches into the batter.

4 Pour batter into 12 greased or paper-lined muffin cups and bake 20-22 minutes, or until a toothpick inserted into a muffin comes out clean.

Cushman's Tips

The ½ cup of puréed peaches is about the amount of purée you should get from 1 large peach. Simply peel, pit, and then purée in a food processor. The 1 cup of chopped peaches is also about 1 large peach.

Oregold
PEACHES

Peach Turnovers

TOTAL PREPARATION TIME: 45 MINS   DIFFICULTY: HARD   SERVES: 8

There simply is no substitute for a freshly baked turnover. When they are straight out of the oven and warm, it really is a thing of beauty! I find peach turnovers to be especially delicious, as the slight tartness of the peach balances out the sweetness of the filling.

Shopping List

3 peaches, peeled, cored, and sliced

2 tablespoons butter or margarine

½ cup light brown sugar

½ cup sugar

1 teaspoon lemon juice

1 teaspoon apple pie spice

1 tablespoon cornstarch

1 (17.25-ounce) package frozen puffed pastry sheets, thawed

nonstick cooking spray

1 large egg, beaten

coarse sugar, for garnish

1 Combine peaches, butter, brown sugar, sugar, lemon juice, apple pie spice, and cornstarch in a sauté pan over medium-high heat. Bring up to a simmer and cook 3 minutes, just until thickened. Transfer to the freezer to cool down for 15 minutes.

2 Preheat oven to 400 degrees F. Lay out both puffed pastry sheets and slice each into 4 squares.

3 Spoon a spoonful of the chilled peach filling onto each of the pastry squares and then fold over diagonally, pressing to seal. Transfer all 8 turnovers to a large sheet pan greased with non-stick cooking spray.

4 Lightly brush the tops of the turnovers with beaten egg and sprinkle with coarse sugar (if desired).

5 Bake 16-20 minutes, or until pastry is golden brown and filling is just beginning to escape. Let cool 5 minutes before serving warm.

Cushman's Tips

The trick to making a perfect turnover is to get the right amount of filling in each. It really only takes about 3 wedges of peach to fill each turnover, which is about half of what you would instinctively think you need to use.

Southwestern Chicken Salad with Peaches

TOTAL PREPARATION TIME: **20** MINS   DIFFICULTY: EASY   SERVES: **4**

This quick and easy salad with chicken and peaches is also loaded with southwestern toppings like tomato, corn, black beans, bell pepper, onion, and crumbled tortilla chips. The dressing is a simple southwestern ranch made with ranch dressing, salsa, and just a touch of honey to complement the peaches.

Shopping List

1 bag fancy lettuce mix
2 peaches, cut into wedges
½ cup diced tomato
¾ cup frozen corn kernels, thawed
¾ cup canned black beans, drained and rinsed
⅓ cup diced green bell pepper
¼ cup diced red onion
10 ounces southwestern seasoned cooked chicken strips
crumbled tortilla chips, for garnish

DRESSING
¾ cup ranch dressing
¼ cup chunky salsa
1 teaspoon honey

1 Split the lettuce equally between 4 bowls.

2 Top the lettuce in each bowl with an equal amount of the peach wedges, diced tomato, corn kernels, black beans, bell pepper, red onion, and cooked chicken strips.

3 Top each salad with a small handful of crumbled tortilla chips.

4 Combine all Dressing ingredients and serve drizzled over each salad.

Cushman's Tips

Southwestern seasoned cooked chicken strips are usually sold by the lunch meat in a refrigerated case.

Oregold
PEACHES

Peachy French Toast Casserole

TOTAL PREPARATION TIME: 50 MINS   DIFFICULTY: EASY   SERVES: 6

This casserole has fresh peaches on the bottom and French toast baked right on top. It's an entire breakfast baked all in one dish! I like to serve it garnished with a dollop of whipped cream.

Shopping List

nonstick cooking spray

4 peaches, cut into wedges

1 teaspoon lemon juice

½ teaspoon ground cinnamon

½ cup light brown sugar

5 large eggs

1 cup buttermilk

⅓ cup pure maple syrup

1 teaspoon vanilla extract

6 thick slices bread

1 Spray a 13x9 baking dish with non-stick cooking spray.

2 In a mixing bowl, toss peaches in lemon juice and cinnamon. Pour into the bottom of the baking dish.

3 In another mixing bowl, whisk together brown sugar, eggs, buttermilk, maple syrup, and vanilla extract.

4 Dip bread slices in the egg mixture and then arrange slices in a single layer over the peaches in the baking dish. Pour any remaining egg mixture over top all in the baking dish. Cover and refrigerate for at least 2 hours.

5 Preheat oven to 375 degrees F. Uncover casserole and bake 34-38 minutes, or until the eggs have set and bread is beginning to brown.

Cushman's Tips

You can prepare this as far in advance as the night before to bake for breakfast in the morning.

Oregold
PEACHES

Pork Tenderloin and Peach Salad

TOTAL PREPARATION TIME: **40** MINS   DIFFICULTY: **MEDIUM**   SERVES: **4**

This salad is served with wedges of fresh peach, tomatoes, crumbled gorgonzola cheese, and warm slices of roasted pork tenderloin. The sweetness of the peaches is the perfect complement to the Cajun-spiced pork.

Shopping List

1 pork tenderloin (about 1 ¼ pounds)

¼ teaspoon salt

¼ teaspoon pepper

¼ teaspoon dry thyme

¼ teaspoon paprika

⅛ teaspoon garlic powder

nonstick cooking spray

SALAD

1 bag fancy lettuce mix

2 peaches, cut into wedges

1 cup grape tomatoes, halved

1 cup crumbled gorgonzola cheese

balsamic vinaigrette, to dress

1 Preheat oven to 450 degrees F. In a large mixing bowl, toss pork tenderloin with salt, pepper, thyme, paprika, and garlic powder. Transfer to a sheet pan coated with nonstick cooking spray.

2 Bake 15-20 minutes, or until a meat thermometer registers 145 degrees F. Let rest 10 minutes before carving into thin medallions.

3 Split the lettuce mix equally between 4 bowls.

4 Top the lettuce in each bowl with an equal amount of the peach wedges, tomatoes, and gorgonzola cheese.

5 Top each salad with 6 thin medallions of pork and serve drizzled with balsamic vinaigrette.

Cushman's Tips

To make your own balsamic vinaigrette, blend together 3 tablespoons balsamic vinegar, 1 teaspoon minced garlic, 1 teaspoon Dijon mustard, and ½ cup olive oil, adding salt and pepper to taste.

Peach Bottom Pancakes

TOTAL PREPARATION TIME: 30 MINS   **DIFFICULTY: Easy**   **SERVES: 4**

These pancakes have a whole lotta' peaches griddled right into them. The secret to keeping them held together is adding the peaches not to the batter, but to the pancake itself after it has already formed on the griddle.

Shopping List

⅔ cup milk

1 large egg

2 tablespoons butter, melted

1 cup all-purpose flour

¼ cup sugar

2 teaspoons baking powder

½ teaspoon salt

¼ teaspoon cinnamon

1 tablespoon butter or margarine (for the skillet)

2 small peaches, peeled and finely chopped

maple syrup or honey

1 In a mixing bowl, whisk together milk, egg, and butter.

2 In a separate mixing bowl, combine flour, sugar, baking powder, salt, and cinnamon.

3 Whisk the wet ingredients into the dry ingredients, just until combined.

4 Place 1 tablespoon of butter in a large nonstick skillet or on a griddle over medium-high heat, heating until melted.

5 Use an ice cream scooper to scoop batter, and release onto the hot pan to create the pancakes. Add as many to the pan as will fit.

6 Once batter has spread out and is beginning to cook, sprinkle a generous amount of chopped peaches over top of each.

7 Flip pancakes once air bubbles begin to surface. Cook until both sides are golden brown, lowering the heat if they begin to brown too quickly.

8 Repeat steps 4-7 until all batter is used. Serve drizzled with maple syrup or honey.

Slow Cooker Peach Pork Chops

TOTAL PREPARATION TIME: **6+ HRS**   DIFFICULTY: **EASY**   SERVES: **6**

These thick-cut pork chops are slow cooked in a sweet and somewhat spicy peach barbecue sauce with just a small touch of cinnamon to make things interesting.

Shopping List

4 thick pork chops (about 1-inch thick)

salt and pepper

1 tablespoon vegetable oil

3 peaches, peeled and cut into wedges

¼ cup apple juice

2 tablespoons light brown sugar

1 cup prepared barbecue sauce

3 tablespoons cider vinegar

⅛ teaspoon ground cinnamon

⅛ teaspoon crushed red pepper flakes

¼ teaspoon salt

1 Season both sides of pork chops with salt and pepper. Add oil and chops to a large skillet over medium-high heat and brown lightly on both sides, about 3-4 minutes per side.

2 Transfer browned pork chops to a slow cooker set to low and place peach wedges on top.

3 Whisk together all remaining ingredients and pour over peaches and pork in slow cooker.

4 Cover and cook for 6-7 hours, or until pork chops are tender. Mash peaches into the sauce before serving.

Cushman's Tips

You can make this with bone-in or boneless pork chops, whichever is your preference.

Oregold
PEACHES

Grilled Peach Chicken

TOTAL PREPARATION TIME: 30 MINS   DIFFICULTY: EASY   SERVES: 4

I love grilling peaches, as the smoky charred taste of the grill cuts their sweetness perfectly. Serving the grilled peaches atop peach marinated chicken makes for an entrée that is packed with fresh peach flavor.

Shopping List

1 peach, pitted and puréed

¼ cup soy sauce

1 tablespoon honey

1 tablespoon vegetable oil

1 teaspoon minced garlic

¼ teaspoon dry oregano

4 boneless, skinless chicken breasts

2 peaches, cut into wedges

2 teaspoons vegetable oil

1 In a mixing bowl, combine puréed peach, soy sauce, honey, vegetable oil, garlic, and oregano. Add chicken breasts and refrigerate for at least 3 hours to marinate.

2 Preheat a grill, indoor grill, or grill pan to high. Remove chicken from marinade and grill until cooked through, about 4-5 minutes on each side.

3 Toss peach wedges in the 2 teaspoons of vegetable oil and grill alongside chicken, about 2 minutes on each side, just until well "marked" by the grill.

4 Serve each grilled chicken breast topped with a few grilled peach wedges.

Cushman's Tips

You can also slice the chicken after grilling and thread onto bamboo skewers along with the grilled peach wedges to make a very unique party appetizer!

Ginger Peach Chicken Breasts

TOTAL PREPARATION TIME: 45 MINS   **DIFFICULTY: EASY**   **SERVES: 6**

Ginger and peaches are a wonderful combination that is illustrated here in this very simple recipe for baked chicken breasts. Serve over white rice and alongside green vegetables for a complete meal.

Shopping List

nonstick cooking spray

6 boneless, skinless chicken breasts

1 tablespoon vegetable oil

salt and pepper

3 peaches, peeled and cut into wedges

¼ cup light brown sugar

¼ teaspoon ground ginger

1 tablespoon butter, melted

2 tablespoons lemon juice

1 teaspoon cornstarch

1 Preheat oven to 350 degrees F. Spray a 13x9 baking dish with nonstick cooking spray.

2 Toss chicken in vegetable oil and place in baking dish. Season with a generous amount of salt and pepper.

3 In a large mixing bowl, toss together all remaining ingredients and pour over the chicken in the baking dish.

4 Bake 30 minutes, or until cutting into the thickest piece of chicken reveals no pink. Serve smothered in peaches and juices from the baking dish.

Cushman's Tips

For an even better flavor, substitute 1 tablespoon of grated fresh ginger root in place of the ground ginger used in this recipe.

Barbecue Peach Glazed Salmon

TOTAL PREPARATION TIME: **25** MINS   DIFFICULTY: EASY   SERVES: **4**

While this salmon is topped with a delicious (and simple!) Barbecue Peach Glaze, there's no need to fire up the barbecue grill. I find grilling fish with sweet sauces like this one to be quite a sticky situation, so I simply oven roast the flavors to perfection instead!

Shopping List

1 ½ pounds salmon, cut into 4 fillets

1 tablespoon olive oil

¼ teaspoon salt

⅛ teaspoon pepper

½ cup barbecue sauce

½ cup puréed peaches

1 teaspoon honey

⅛ teaspoon onion powder

1 Preheat oven to 400 degrees F. Toss salmon fillets in oil, salt, and pepper and place on an aluminum foil lined sheet pan.

2 In a mixing bowl, whisk together all remaining ingredients to create a glaze.

3 Spread an equal amount of the glaze over each salmon fillet.

4 Bake 15-20 minutes, or until salmon is opaque and easily flaked with a fork. Serve immediately.

Cushman's Tips

For even more peachy flavor, try serving this topped with grilled peach wedges in the same way that you serve my Grilled Peach Chicken, recipe page: 143.

Peach Ice Cream

TOTAL PREPARATION TIME: 30 MINS   DIFFICULTY: MEDIUM   SERVES: 8

My ice cream maker is one of my favorite kitchen gadgets, especially when it comes to preparing fruit filled ice creams like this one. I could write a whole book of ice cream recipes, but this Peach Ice Cream is definitely at the top of the heap. It's the addition of almond extract to the more standard vanilla extract and ground cinnamon that really makes this shine! Almonds and peaches come from the same family, so a little almond extract always brightens up the flavor of peaches.

Shopping List

3 large peaches, peeled and pitted

3 cups heavy cream

1 cup milk

1 cup sugar

1 teaspoon vanilla extract

¼ teaspoon almond extract

¼ teaspoon ground cinnamon

1 In a food processor, purée 2 of the peaches until smooth. Roughly chop the remaining peach and set aside.

2 In a large mixing bowl, whisk the peach purée into the heavy cream, milk, sugar, vanilla extract, almond extract, and ground cinnamon to create the ice cream base. Whisk until all sugar is dissolved.

3 Fold the chopped peaches into the ice cream base.

4 Place the finished mixture into the bowl of an ice cream maker and churn according to the manufacturer's directions. Serve garnished with a fresh peach wedge.

Cushman's Tips

The easiest way to peel the peaches is to simply drop them into boiling water for 30 seconds. Once removed and cooled, the peel should simply slide right off!

Poached Peaches with Yogurt

TOTAL PREPARATION TIME: 20 MINS   DIFFICULTY: EASY   SERVES: 4

These poached peach halves in syrup are an easy but elegant dessert that is easily prepared in advance. They are topped with vanilla yogurt and a sprinkling of cinnamon and sugar, so if you are lucky enough to have a small kitchen torch, I would definitely recommend lightly caramelizing the sugar just before serving.

Shopping List

1 cup sugar

1 cup apple juice

1 cup water

½ teaspoon pure almond extract

4 peaches, halved and pitted

2 cups vanilla yogurt

¼ cup light brown sugar

¼ teaspoon ground cinnamon

1 Place sugar, apple juice, water, and almond extract in a large nonstick skillet over medium heat and bring up to a simmer.

2 Place peaches face down in the skillet and cook 6-7 minutes, or until tender.

3 Remove from heat and transfer to a large food storage container. Refrigerate until fully chilled, about 4 hours.

4 Place 2 chilled peach halves in each of 4 serving bowls. Drizzle with a spoonful of the chilled poaching liquid.

5 Place a large scoop of vanilla yogurt over the peaches in each bowl.

6 Combine brown sugar and cinnamon and sprinkle over the yogurt in each bowl. Serve immediately.

Cushman's Tips

This is also absolutely delicious when served topped with crunchy granola clusters.

Peach Sorbet

TOTAL PREPARATION TIME: 20 MINS   DIFFICULTY: MEDIUM   SERVES: 4

Like my Mango Peach Smoothies, recipe page: 131, this is one of my go-to recipes when I have a surplus of peaches that are over-ripening. I would highly recommend making this in an ice cream maker, but if you do not have one, you can simply freeze in individual serving dishes. The texture won't be as silky smooth as when made using an ice cream maker but more like the texture of Italian ice.

Shopping List

⅔ cup water

½ cup sugar

1 tablespoon lemon juice

4 peaches, peeled and chopped

1 Add water, sugar, and lemon juice to a sauce pot over medium-high heat and bring to a boil. Let cook 2 minutes, just until sugar has dissolved.

2 Remove from heat and let cool at least 15 minutes.

3 Place sugar mixture in a food processor or blender and then add peaches. Pulse or blend until peaches are entirely puréed into the mixture.

4 Place the finished mixture into the bowl of an ice cream maker and churn according to the manufacturer's directions.

Cushman's Tips

*A*dding 1 tablespoon of a peach flavored liqueur, such as peach schnapps, will not only add more peach flavor but also help keep the sorbet soft and silky in the freezer as alcohol does not freeze.

Maple Peach Cobbler

TOTAL PREPARATION TIME: **1** HOUR   DIFFICULTY: EASY   SERVES: **6**

Whether this recipe is technically a "cobbler" or a "crisp" I can't say for sure—but I do know that the crunchy oat topping is absolutely delicious! The real trick to this recipe is using "pure" maple syrup and not the artificially flavored pancake syrup; the taste is most definitely worth the premium in price.

Shopping List

nonstick cooking spray

6 cups peeled and sliced peaches

¼ cup pure maple syrup

½ cup sugar

2 tablespoons all-purpose flour

2 teaspoons cornstarch

½ teaspoon ground cinnamon

TOPPING

¾ cup old-fashioned oats

⅓ cup sugar

½ cup all-purpose flour

4 tablespoons butter or margarine, melted

2 tablespoons pure maple syrup

½ teaspoon cinnamon

1 Preheat oven to 375 degrees F. Spray an 8x8 baking dish with nonstick cooking spray.

2 In a large mixing bowl, combine peaches, maple syrup, sugar, flour, cornstarch, and cinnamon, and pour into the greased baking dish.

3 In a separate bowl, combine all Topping ingredients, and using a large spoon, drop over top the fruit mixture in the baking dish.

4 Bake for 45 minutes, or until bubbly hot and the topping has begun to brown. Let cool for at least 5 minutes before spooning into serving bowls.

Cushman's Tips

The easiest way to peel the peaches is to simply drop them into boiling water for 30 seconds. Once removed and cooled, the peel should simply slide right off!

Honeycrisp Apples

Appetizers

Creamy Cheddar Apple Dip 155

Breakfast and Lunches

Apple and Cream Cheese Pastry Pockets 157
Waldorf Salad 158
Apple and Sage Sausage Patties 159
Apple Raisin Bread 161
Turkey and Apple Wraps 163
Apple Pie Oatmeal 164

Main Courses and Sides

Slow Cooker Cranberry Apple Pork Roast 165
Bratwurst with Apple Kraut 167
Apple and Caramelized Onion Pork Chops 168
Roast Turkey Breast with Apples 169
Apple and Cheddar Stuffed Chicken Breasts 171
Scalloped Apples 172
Rice Pilaf with Apples and Almonds 173

Desserts

Apple Walnut Bars 174
Apple Tart 175
Cranberry Apple Crisp 176
No Sugar Added Apple Pie 177
Caramel Apples 179
Apple Cinnamon Dessert Pizza 181
Apple Dumplings 182
Apple Cinnamon Cookies 183
Apple Pie 185

Creamy Cheddar Apple Dip

TOTAL PREPARATION TIME: 10 MINS   DIFFICULTY: EASY   SERVES: 8

This cheesy dip is tangy and sharp, which is the perfect contrast to sweet, crunchy apple wedges. A great alternative to potato chips and dip, this recipe is really great for potlucks and get-togethers. I find that it is best served at room temperature so there is no need to worry about reheating.

Shopping List

8 ounces light cream cheese

3 tablespoons apple juice

1 tablespoon finely minced green onion

1 teaspoon minced garlic

½ teaspoon Worcestershire sauce

¼ teaspoon paprika

¼ teaspoon ground mustard

1 teaspoon sugar

¼ teaspoon salt

1 cup shredded sharp Cheddar cheese

apple wedges, for dipping

1 Place all ingredients, except Cheddar cheese and apple wedges, in a microwave-safe bowl.

2 Microwave on high for 1 ½ minutes. Stir well.

3 Microwave an additional 30 seconds.

4 Stir in Cheddar cheese and microwave an additional 45 seconds. Stir until all is combined. Let cool 10-15 minutes and serve at room temperature. Serve alongside plenty of fresh apple wedges for dipping.

Cushman's Tips

The sharper the Cheddar cheese, the better, so I suggest purchasing a brick of "extra sharp" Cheddar and shredding it yourself rather than buying a bag of the more mild pre-shredded cheese.

Apple and Cream Cheese Pastry Pockets

TOTAL PREPARATION TIME: **45** MINS   DIFFICULTY: **HARD**   SERVES: **8**

These pastry pockets are filled with hot cinnamon apples and warm, gooey cream cheese and topped with a crunchy almond streusel-like topping that can't be beat.

Shopping List

1 large apple, peeled and diced

3 tablespoons light brown sugar

¼ teaspoon apple pie spice

1 ½ teaspoons cornstarch

1 (17.25-ounce) package frozen puffed pastry sheets, thawed

4 ounces light cream cheese

nonstick cooking spray

ALMOND TOPPING

¼ cup raw almonds

¼ cup all-purpose flour

¼ cup sugar

3 tablespoons butter, cold

1 Combine diced apple, brown sugar, apple pie spice, and cornstarch, and microwave on high for 1 minute. Stir and microwave an additional 45 seconds, or until mixture is very thick. Transfer to the freezer to cool down for 15 minutes.

2 Preheat oven to 400 degrees F. Lay out both puffed pastry sheets and slice each into 4 squares, or use a round pastry cutter to cut each sheet into 4 circles.

3 Cut cream cheese into 8 equal portions and place onto each of the 8 pastry squares. Cover cream cheese with a spoonful of the chilled apple filling and then fold pastry over diagonally, pressing to seal. Transfer all 8 pastries to a large sheet pan greased with nonstick cooking spray.

4 Place all Almond Topping ingredients in a food processor and pulse until coarse and crumbly.

5 Top each pastry pocket with a large spoonful of the crumbled Almond Topping.

6 Bake 16-20 minutes, or until pastry is golden brown and filling is just beginning to escape. Let cool 5 minutes before serving warm.

Cushman's Tips

You can also make these without the Almond Topping if you would prefer. Still delicious, they are just a whole lot easier to prepare that way.

Honeycrisp
APPLES

Waldorf Salad

TOTAL PREPARATION TIME: 15 MINS   **DIFFICULTY: EASY**   **SERVES: 6**

This is a great picnic salad that is often overlooked. Sweet Honeycrisp apples are the perfect choice to offset the creamy mayonnaise and earthy walnuts that, along with celery, are the classic components of this sweet and savory salad.

Shopping List

½ cup mayonnaise (may use light)

2 teaspoons lemon juice

½ teaspoon sugar

⅛ teaspoon celery salt

⅛ teaspoon nutmeg

2 apples, cored and chopped

2 stalks celery, diced

½ cup chopped walnuts

1 In a mixing bowl, combine mayonnaise, lemon juice, sugar, celery salt, and nutmeg to create the dressing.

2 Fold apples, celery, and walnuts into the dressing mixture.

3 For best taste, refrigerate for 30 minutes to let the flavors combine. Serve chilled.

Cushman's Tips

The lemon juice in the dressing will help keep the cut apples from oxidizing and turning brown in your salad.

Honeycrisp
APPLES

Apple and Sage Sausage Patties

TOTAL PREPARATION TIME: 20 MINS   DIFFICULTY: EASY   SERVES: 4

These breakfast sausage patties have fresh minced apples and chopped sage throughout. The sweet apples are a great way to cut the saltiness of the pork sausage.

Shopping List

1 tablespoon butter or margarine

½ cup finely minced apple

2 green onions, finely chopped

4 fresh sage leaves, finely chopped

1 pound ground pork sausage

1 tablespoon vegetable oil

1 Place butter and apples in a skillet over medium-high heat and sauté for 2-3 minutes, or until apple has softened.

2 Add green onions and chopped sage to the pan and continue sautéing for 1 minute. Remove from heat and let cool at least 5 minutes.

3 In a mixing bowl, fold apple mixture into the ground pork sausage, kneading until all is well combined.

4 Form sausage mixture into 8 round patties.

5 Place vegetable oil in a skillet over medium-high heat. Add sausage patties and cook until well browned on both sides and fully cooked throughout, about 5 minutes on each side.

Cushman's Tips

The pork sausage that is best for this recipe is the kind that looks like ground beef and usually comes in pinched tubes in a refrigerated case.

Honeycrisp
APPLES

Apple Raisin Bread

TOTAL PREPARATION TIME: 2 HRS   DIFFICULTY: HARD   SERVES: 8

This cinnamon apple and raisin filled bread is amazingly light and fluffy and has just the right amount of sweetness. You'd swear it was made in a bread machine, but I just make it in my ordinary oven!

Shopping List

1 (.25-ounce) envelope active dry yeast
1 teaspoon sugar
½ cup warm water
nonstick cooking spray

WET INGREDIENTS

1 large egg, beaten
⅓ cup applesauce
¼ cup vegetable oil
⅓ cup light brown sugar

DRY INGREDIENTS

3 cups all-purpose flour
½ teaspoon salt

APPLE INGREDIENTS

1 apple, peeled, cored, and finely diced
½ cup raisins
¼ cup light brown sugar
1 teaspoon ground cinnamon
1 teaspoon lemon juice

1 Stir yeast and sugar into the warm water and let sit 15 minutes.

2 In 3 separate mixing bowls combine the 3 sets of ingredients: a different bowl for the Wet, Dry, and Apple Ingredients.

3 Add yeast mixture and Wet Ingredients to the Dry Ingredients. Knead with your hands until a ball of dough is formed. Place ball of dough in a large bowl that has been sprayed with nonstick cooking spray. Cover with plastic wrap and let sit in a warm place to rise for about 1 hour, or until doubled.

4 Drain any excess liquid from the Apple Ingredients mixture and then knead into the risen dough until mostly combined. Place into a 9x5 loaf pan sprayed with nonstick cooking spray. Cover with plastic wrap and let rise another 45 minutes.

5 Preheat oven to 350 degrees F. Place loaf in oven and bake 30-35 minutes, or until bread is springy and the top crust is a nice, dark brown. Let cool at least 15 minutes before slicing and serving warm or room temperature.

Cushman's Tips

For the best looking loaf of bread with a nice brown crust, lightly brush the top of the loaf with beaten egg before baking.

Honeycrisp
APPLES

Turkey and Apple Wraps

TOTAL PREPARATION TIME: 20 MINS   DIFFICULTY: EASY   SERVES: 4

These Turkey and Apple Wraps are smothered with a delicious cranberry cream cheese spread and filled with not only turkey and apples but also walnuts and fresh spinach leaves as well. Though I usually make this with sliced turkey from the deli counter, this is also a great way to use roasted turkey leftovers.

Shopping List

¼ cup sweetened dried cranberries

3 tablespoons milk

8 ounces light cream cheese

4 flour tortillas

½ cup chopped walnuts

1 pound sliced deli turkey breast

2 apples, julienned

2 cups fresh baby spinach leaves

1 In the bowl of a food processor, let dried cranberries soak in milk for at least 15 minutes.

2 Add the cream cheese to the milk and cranberries and pulse until fully combined, about 1 minute.

3 Lay the 4 tortillas out and spread an equal amount of the cranberry cream cheese spread across the surface of each.

4 Top the cream cheese spread on each tortilla with an equal amount of the chopped walnuts, then sliced turkey, then julienned apples, and then spinach leaves.

5 Roll each tortilla up as tight as possible, seam side down. Slice each in half and serve.

Cushman's Tips

*Y*ou can make these into a very healthy lunch by substituting fat-free cream cheese in place of the light cream cheese and using whole wheat tortillas in place of the white.

Honeycrisp
APPLES

Apple Pie Oatmeal

TOTAL PREPARATION TIME: 10 MINS   **DIFFICULTY: EASY**   **SERVES: 3**

This simple microwave oatmeal recipe with cinnamon and diced apples is made from whole rolled oats in only 5 minutes. It's so easy that I have to wonder why they even need to make instant oatmeal.

Shopping List

1 large apple, peeled and diced

1 ¼ cups rolled oats

1 cup water

¾ cup milk

2 tablespoons butter or margarine

3 tablespoons light brown sugar

½ teaspoon ground cinnamon

⅛ teaspoon ground nutmeg

additional brown sugar, for garnish

1 Place all ingredients in a microwave-safe bowl and stir to combine.

2 Microwave on high for 4-5 minutes, or until hot and bubbly.

3 Let cool 5 minutes before serving sprinkled with additional brown sugar.

Cushman's Tips

You can also make this with fewer calories by substituting your favorite sugar substitute in place of the light brown sugar. I would suggest stirring it in after cooking, as some sugar substitutes lose their sweetness once cooked.

Honeycrisp APPLES

Slow Cooker Cranberry Apple Pork Roast

TOTAL PREPARATION TIME: 7+ HRS   **DIFFICULTY: EASY**   **SERVES: 6**

This pork roast with a sweet and tart cranberry and apple sauce is effortlessly prepared in a slow cooker with minimal ingredients. Carve the roast whole or shred and serve over top savory rice or potatoes.

Shopping List

1 pork roast, about 3-4 pounds

salt and pepper

onion powder

1 (14-ounce) can whole berry cranberry sauce

3 tablespoons light brown sugar

½ cup apple juice

2 apples, peeled, cored, and chopped

1 teaspoon orange zest

1 teaspoon minced garlic

1 Season pork roast with a generous amount of salt, pepper, and onion powder and place in a slow cooker set to low.

2 Add all remaining ingredients to the slow cooker.

3 Cover and cook for 7-8 hours, or until pork is tender.

Cushman's Tips

For the best flavor, season the sauce with salt to taste before serving. The salt will help enhance the sweet and tart flavors of the sauce.

Bratwurst with Apple Kraut

TOTAL PREPARATION TIME: 25 MINS   DIFFICULTY: EASY   SERVES: 5-6

Everybody knows that bratwurst, beer, and sauerkraut go wonderfully together, but adding sweet honeycrisp apples to the equation truly offsets the stronger, more acidic flavors of the beer and sauerkraut. Serve just as is or piled into hoagie rolls and topped with mustard.

Shopping List

5-6 bratwurst

1 tablespoon vegetable oil

1 cup beer

2 tablespoons butter or margarine

2 apples, julienned

1 pound sauerkraut, drained and rinsed

1 tablespoon light brown sugar

1 tablespoon flour

1 Place bratwurst and vegetable oil in a skillet over medium-high heat and brown sausages on all sides.

2 Add beer, cover, reduce heat to medium, and let simmer for 10 minutes.

3 Add butter and julienned apples, and toss until butter is melted and apples begin to sweat.

4 In a mixing bowl, combine drained sauerkraut, light brown sugar, and flour, tossing until no clumps of flour remain.

5 Stir sauerkraut mixture into the skillet and bring everything back up to a simmer. Let simmer 3 minutes before serving.

Cushman's Tips

You can prepare this with precooked or raw bratwurst; both will work just fine. If starting with raw bratwurst, be sure to cut into one to test for doneness before serving.

Apple and Caramelized Onion Pork Chops

TOTAL PREPARATION TIME: **1 HOUR**   DIFFICULTY: **EASY**   SERVES: **6**

These pork chops with apple wedges and caramelized onions bake nice and tender in a sweet and tangy sauce. Serve alongside mashed potatoes or roasted potato wedges for the perfect family meal!

Shopping List

4 apples, cored and cut into wedges

3 tablespoons butter or margarine

2 yellow onions, sliced

1 tablespoon all-purpose flour

1 cup apple juice

1 tablespoon vinegar

1 tablespoon light brown sugar

1 teaspoon minced garlic

1 tablespoon vegetable oil

6 pork chops, about ¾ inch thick

salt and pepper

1 Preheat oven to 350 degrees F. Spread apple wedges across the bottom of a 13x9 baking dish.

2 Place butter and onions in a large skillet over medium-high heat and sauté until onions begin to caramelize, about 8 minutes.

3 Whisk together flour, apple juice, vinegar, brown sugar, and minced garlic and pour into the skillet. Bring up

to a simmer and then remove from heat. Pour onions and sauce over the apples in the baking dish.

4 Wipe skillet clean and return to medium-high heat. Add vegetable oil to the skillet.

5 Season both sides of pork chops with salt and pepper and add to the skillet, lightly browning on both sides.

6 Arrange browned pork chops atop the apples, onions, and sauce in the baking dish. Cover and bake for 40 minutes, or until pork chops are tender and white throughout.

Cushman's Tips

You can use pork chops with or without bones in this recipe, whichever is your preference.

Honeycrisp
APPLES

Roast Turkey Breast with Apples

TOTAL PREPARATION TIME: 3 HRS   DIFFICULTY: MEDIUM   SERVES: 8

Roasted turkey breast is something I like to make at least a few times a year, as it is easier than roasting an entire turkey but still creates a good amount of leftovers. And leftovers are definitely something you will want to have when it comes to this moist and delicious recipe.

Shopping List

1 whole turkey breast, about 5-6 pounds

1 apple, cored and cut into wedges

4 tablespoons butter, softened

1 teaspoon salt

¾ teaspoon apple pie spice

¼ teaspoon pepper

APPLES

3 apples, cored and cut into wedges

2 tablespoons butter or margarine, melted

3 tablespoons light brown sugar

1 tablespoon apple juice

1 Preheat oven to 325 degrees F. Place turkey breast in a large roasting pan. Stuff apple into the turkey cavity.

2 Using a heavy spoon, mash together softened butter, salt, apple pie spice, and pepper. Spread the butter over every surface of the turkey skin.

3 Bake uncovered for 90 minutes, covering with aluminum foil if skin gets too browned.

4 In a mixing bowl, combine all Apple ingredients. Using a slotted spoon, transfer apple mixture to the roasting pan, entirely surrounding the roasted turkey.

5 Pour liquid from the bottom of the mixing bowl over top of turkey, cover with aluminum foil, and bake an additional 30-50 minutes, or until a meat thermometer inserted into the thickest part registers 185 degrees F. Let turkey rest several minutes before carving and serving alongside apples and juices from the pan.

Cushman's Tips

I would definitely recommend using a digital kitchen thermometer with a probe that you can insert into the turkey and leave in for the entire roasting time. This way, you know the exact moment when it is done and don't have to constantly recheck for temperature.

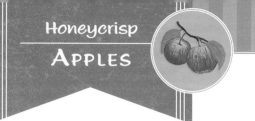

Honeycrisp
APPLES

Apple and Cheddar Stuffed Chicken Breasts

TOTAL PREPARATION TIME: 35 MINS   **DIFFICULTY: MEDIUM**   **SERVES: 4**

Apples and cheese are most definitely a winning combination, especially in this stuffed chicken breast recipe. I prefer fresh chopped sage in the stuffing, but you can also use a pinch of dried thyme or Italian seasoning to save a little money.

Shopping List

4 boneless, skinless chicken breasts

1 tablespoon vegetable oil

¼ teaspoon salt

⅛ teaspoon black pepper

1 cup shredded sharp Cheddar cheese

½ cup finely diced apple

2 teaspoons minced garlic

4 fresh sage leaves, chopped

toothpicks

2 cups Italian breadcrumbs

2 large eggs, beaten

nonstick cooking spray

1 Preheat the oven to 400 degrees F. Place chicken breasts between two sheets of plastic wrap and pound with a meat mallet or rolling pin until flattened and about ⅓ inch thick.

2 Place pounded chicken breasts in a mixing bowl and cover with vegetable oil, salt, and pepper. Toss until chicken is well coated.

3 In another mixing bowl, combine Cheddar cheese, apple, garlic, and sage to make the stuffing.

4 Place pounded and seasoned chicken breasts on a sheet pan. Spoon ¼ of the apple filling onto each chicken breast and tuck the sides of the breast up and over it. Secure with toothpicks.

5 Dip each stuffed breast in breadcrumbs, then beaten egg, and then back into the breadcrumbs to fully coat.

6 Place breaded chicken breasts on a sheet pan greased with nonstick cooking spray. Bake 20 minutes, or until slicing into one of the breasts reveals no pink. Let cool 5 minutes before serving.

Cushman's Tips

This is also very good with Swiss or Fontina cheese, but Cheddar is easiest as you can purchase it pre-shredded.

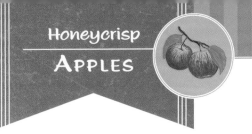

Scalloped Apples

TOTAL PREPARATION TIME: **15** MINS   DIFFICULTY: **EASY**   SERVES: **8**

I like to serve these Scalloped Apples as a side dish at picnics and barbecues. Though they are quite sweet and a whole lot like the filling of an apple pie, this is a pretty traditional southern side dish served right alongside a main course! I will admit that making them in the microwave as I do isn't traditional, but I find it too easy to resist!

Shopping List

5 large apples, peeled

¼ cup sugar

2 tablespoons light brown sugar

2 tablespoons butter or margarine

2 tablespoons cornstarch

¾ teaspoon ground cinnamon

⅛ teaspoon ground nutmeg

1 Slice apples into thin wedges and place in a microwave-safe bowl.

2 Cover apples with all remaining ingredients and toss to combine.

3 Cover bowl with plastic wrap and poke a small hole to vent. Microwave on high for 4 minutes.

4 Stir well and microwave an additional 3-5 minutes, or until apples are tender. Serve hot.

Cushman's Tips

*Y*ou can also toss in a handful of sweetened dried cranberries before cooking to add a little more tartness to this dish.

Honeycrisp
APPLES

Rice Pilaf with Apples and Almonds

TOTAL PREPARATION TIME: 30 MINS   DIFFICULTY: EASY   SERVES: 4

This easy rice pilaf with diced apples and toasted almond slivers is a great side dish for roasted meat like pork, chicken, or turkey. Speaking of turkey, around the holidays I make this with an added pinch of allspice stirred in for a little more festive flavor.

Shopping List

1 tablespoon vegetable oil

1 cup dry long grain rice

1 tablespoon powdered onion soup mix

⅛ teaspoon poultry seasoning

⅛ teaspoon pepper

1 ⅔ cups low-sodium chicken broth

1 cup finely diced apple

⅓ cup slivered almonds, toasted

1 Place vegetable oil and rice in a pot over medium-high heat and cook, stirring constantly, for 2 minutes.

2 Add soup mix, poultry seasoning, pepper, and chicken broth to the pot and stir to combine.

3 Bring up to a boil and then reduce heat to low. Cover and let simmer 12 minutes.

4 Add diced apples to the rice, re-cover, and let cook an additional 4 minutes.

5 Remove from heat and let sit 5 minutes before stirring in toasted almonds and serving.

Cushman's Tips

To toast slivered almonds, simply bake at 350 degrees F. for 8-14 minutes, just until light brown and aromatic.

Apple Walnut Bars

TOTAL PREPARATION TIME: 1 HOUR **DIFFICULTY: Easy** **SERVES: 9**

These Apple Walnut Bars are somewhat chewy like a brownie, somewhat soft like a cake, and crispy around the edges like a cookie.

Shopping List

nonstick cooking spray

1 stick butter or margarine, melted

⅔ cup light brown sugar

½ cup sugar

1 large egg

½ teaspoon vanilla extract

1 cup all-purpose flour

1 teaspoon baking powder

1 teaspoon apple pie spice

1 cup finely diced apple

1 cup chopped walnuts

1 Preheat oven to 350 degrees F. Spray an 8x8 baking dish with nonstick cooking spray.

2 In an electric mixer, combine butter, brown sugar, sugar, egg, and vanilla extract.

3 Add flour, baking powder, and apple pie spice to the mixture and beat for about 1 minute, or until all is well combined. Fold in diced apple and walnuts.

4 Pour batter into the greased baking dish and bake 40 minutes, or until a toothpick inserted into the center comes out mostly clean. Let cool at least 5 minutes before cutting into 9 squares.

Cushman's Tips

These are extremely good when slightly soft and under-baked, as they will have a chewier, more brownie-like consistency.

Honeycrisp
APPLES

Apple Tart

TOTAL PREPARATION TIME: 1 ½ HRS   DIFFICULTY: MEDIUM   SERVES: 8

This beautiful Apple Tart is baked upside down and then flipped out onto a serving platter for presentation. By making it this way you get a nice flat top with fruit that is perfectly caramelized.

Shopping List

¾ cup light brown sugar

¼ cup sugar

3 tablespoons all-purpose flour

¾ teaspoon ground cinnamon

2 tablespoons butter or margarine

4 apples, peeled, cored, and thinly sliced

1 9-inch refrigerated pie crust, thawed

1 Preheat oven to 400 degrees F. Heat brown sugar in a saucepan over medium heat, stirring constantly, until sugar melts. Pour into a 10-inch pie plate.

2 In a food processor, combine sugar, flour, cinnamon, and butter, pulsing until combined and crumbly.

3 Arrange the sliced apples, overlapping each other, in a circular pattern over top the melted brown sugar in the pie plate.

4 Once you have a full layer of apples at the bottom of the pie plate, top all with the crumbly sugar and flour mixture.

5 Create a second layer of overlapping apple slices and then top all with the thawed pie crust, placed flat on top of the apples without touching the sides of the pie plate.

6 Bake 45-50 minutes, or until crust is a deep golden brown. Remove from oven and invert pie plate onto serving platter, releasing the tart. Let cool before slicing.

Cushman's Tips

*Y*ou must flip the tart out of the pie plate while it is still hot, otherwise the sugars may stick to the dish and the tart will never come out.

Cranberry Apple Crisp

TOTAL PREPARATION TIME: **1** HOUR   DIFFICULTY: EASY   SERVES: **6**

This crisp makes a perfect and perfectly easy holiday dessert that you can whip up in advance, wrap, and then bake when you and your guests are ready. Serve topped with ice cream or follow my tips at the bottom of the page to serve this exactly the way I do!

Shopping List

nonstick cooking spray
6 cups peeled and sliced apples
½ cup sweetened dried cranberries
2 teaspoons lemon juice
¼ cup sugar
¼ cup light brown sugar
2 teaspoons cornstarch
2 teaspoons all-purpose flour
1 teaspoon ground cinnamon
1 teaspoon finely grated orange or HoneyBell zest

TOPPING

1 cup vanilla wafer cookies
¼ cup sugar
3 tablespoons butter, cold

1 Preheat oven to 375 degrees F. Spray an 8x8 baking dish with nonstick cooking spray.

2 In a large mixing bowl, combine apples, dried cranberries, lemon juice, sugar, brown sugar, cornstarch, flour, cinnamon, and orange zest, and pour into the greased baking dish.

3 In a food processor, combine all Topping ingredients and pulse just until cookies are crumbled and butter is chopped and dispersed throughout.

4 Drop Topping by the large spoonful over top of the fruit mixture in the baking dish.

5 Bake for 40-45 minutes, or until bubbly hot and the topping is crisp. Let cool for at least 5 minutes before spooning into serving bowls.

Cushman's Tips

Believe it or not, I love to serve this topped with lemon sorbet or sherbert instead of ice cream! The tart lemon goes really great with the sweet apples and tart cranberries.

No Sugar Added Apple Pie

TOTAL PREPARATION TIME: 1 ½ HRS   **DIFFICULTY: MEDIUM**   **SERVES: 8**

I invited a very good friend, who is diabetic, to a holiday get together one year and decided to try my hand at preparing an apple pie without any added sugar. I made both this pie for my friend and a regular apple pie for my other guests, and let me tell you... not only did my friend love this pie, but he was also convinced that I had mixed it up with the regular sugar-filled pie!

Shopping List

2 9-inch refrigerated pie crusts, thawed

6 cups peeled and sliced apple

1 cup bulk sugar substitute

2 ½ tablespoons cornstarch

1 ¼ teaspoons apple pie spice

¼ teaspoon vanilla extract

⅛ teaspoon salt

1 large egg, beaten

1 Preheat oven to 425 degrees F.

2 Press 1 pie crust into the bottom of a 9-inch pie plate.

3 In a large mixing bowl, toss together sliced apples, sugar substitute, cornstarch, apple pie spice, vanilla extract, and salt. Pour into the prepared pie crust.

4 Cover pie with remaining crust, crimping edges to fuse the bottom and top crust together. Trim any excess crust around the edges and cut slices in the top crust to vent. Lightly brush with beaten egg.

5 Bake 40-45 minutes, or until filling is bubbly hot and the crust is golden brown.

Cushman's Tips

The "bulk" sugar substitute referenced in this recipe is the kind that is sold in bags or boxes and measures cup for cup the same as sugar.

Caramel Apples

TOTAL PREPARATION TIME: 1 HOUR   **DIFFICULTY: MEDIUM**   **SERVES: 8**

Real Caramel Apples that are made from a homemade caramel sauce are rarely seen these days, as most people have opted to make them by simply melting caramel candies. There is hardly any difference in effort to make everything from scratch, but there is a very, very big difference in flavor.

Shopping List

8 apples

8 popsicle or round wooden sticks

2 packed cups light brown sugar

2 sticks butter

1 (14-ounce) can sweetened condensed milk

1 cup corn syrup

1 cup chopped peanuts, optional

1 Line a sheet pan with wax or parchment paper. Remove stems from apples and insert wooden sticks into their tops, pressing them at least ¾ of the way down into the apple.

2 Place the brown sugar, butter, condensed milk, and corn syrup in a sauce pot over medium-high heat.

3 Cook the caramel mixture, stirring constantly, for 30 minutes, or until a kitchen or candy thermometer registers that the mixture has reached 248 degrees F.

4 Remove caramel from heat and dip apples into it, spinning them to fully coat. Immediately roll the coated apples in the chopped peanuts, pressing lightly to stick.

5 Place the finished candy apples on the lined sheet pan and let cool completely before serving.

Cushman's Tips

The great thing about homemade candy apples is that you can roll them in just about any toppings while they are still warm. There's no need to stick to the classic chopped peanuts! Try rolling in chocolate chips or even crushed pretzels for something completely different.

Apple Cinnamon Dessert Pizza

TOTAL PREPARATION TIME: **45** MINS   DIFFICULTY: MEDIUM   SERVES: **8**

This recipe definitely has more flavors in common with an apple pie or tart than an actual pizza, but the presentation is fun and unique, especially when servings kids. This is the perfect dessert for your next pizza party!

Shopping List

1 large pre-made pizza crust (such as Boboli brand)

2 small apples, peeled, cored, and sliced

1 tablespoon butter or margarine, melted

2 tablespoons sugar

½ teaspoon ground cinnamon

CRUMB TOPPING

½ cup all-purpose flour

½ cup dark brown sugar

4 tablespoons butter or margarine, cold

1 teaspoon ground cinnamon

ICING

1 cup confectioners sugar

1 ½ tablespoons milk

¼ teaspoon vanilla extract

1 Preheat oven to 425 degrees F. Place pizza crust on a large sheet pan.

2 In a large mixing bowl, combine sliced apples, melted butter, sugar, and cinnamon. Toss all to evenly coat, and then spread over the entire surface of the pizza crust.

3 Place all Crumb Topping ingredients in a food processor and pulse until mixture is thick and crumbly. Spoon evenly over the apple covered pizza.

4 Bake 15-20 minutes, or until topping is browned.

5 In a microwave-safe bowl, combine all Icing ingredients and microwave 30 seconds, just until mixture is smooth and somewhat thin. Drizzle evenly over pizza and let cool 2-3 minutes to harden. Slice pizza into 8 slices and serve.

Cushman's Tips

Though Boboli brand pre-made pizza crusts are easiest to find, I actually like to make this recipe with the more plain-looking thin crust pizza crusts that are often sold 2 to a pack.

Apple Dumplings

TOTAL PREPARATION TIME: 1+ HRS   DIFFICULTY: HARD   SERVES: 6

I used to love helping my mother prepare these Apple Dumplings. An entire apple wrapped in a pastry crust and drizzled with a hot, buttery syrup, these are a little more work than an apple pie or cobbler but can be quite fun to prepare.

Shopping List

SAUCE

1 cup apple juice
1 ½ cups water
1 cup sugar
¼ cup light brown sugar
4 tablespoons butter or margarine
¾ teaspoon ground cinnamon

PASTRY

2 cups all-purpose flour
2 teaspoons baking powder
¾ teaspoon salt
¾ cup vegetable shortening
⅓ cup water

DUMPLINGS

6 apples, peeled and cored
6 teaspoons butter or margarine
cinnamon-sugar
nonstick cooking spray

1 Combine all Sauce ingredients in a sauce pot over medium heat. Bring up to a simmer and cook 3 minutes, just until all is melted and combined.

2 Create the Pastry by combining flour, baking powder, and salt. Cut in vegetable shortening until mixture is crumbly, and then add water until a ball of dough is easily formed.

3 On a well-floured surface, separate dough into 6 balls and then roll each out into a 7-inch square.

4 Place a cored apple onto each pastry square and stuff 1 teaspoon of butter into the hole where the core was removed. Sprinkle about ½ teaspoon of cinnamon-sugar over top each apple.

5 Pull the corners of each pastry square up entirely over each apple. Overlap the corners and press them down to seal the apple inside.

6 Preheat oven to 375 degrees F. Spray a 13x9 baking dish with nonstick cooking spray and place the apple dumplings at the bottom. Pour the cooked sauce over top all.

7 Bake 35-40 minutes, or until pastry is a deep golden brown.

Apple Cinnamon Cookies

TOTAL PREPARATION TIME: **25** MINS   DIFFICULTY: EASY   SERVES: **12**

These cakey cookies are stuffed with fresh, crunchy apple and spiced with cinnamon. Soft and delicious, they actually remind me a whole lot of breakfast scones, so feel free to eat these cookies for breakfast! How often do you get permission to do that?

Shopping List

nonstick cooking spray

1 ½ sticks butter or margarine, softened

1 cup sugar

1 large egg

½ teaspoon vanilla extract

2 cups all-purpose flour

2 teaspoons ground cinnamon

1 teaspoon baking powder

1 teaspoon baking soda

1 cup finely diced apple

1 Preheat oven to 375 degrees F. Spray 2 cookie sheets with nonstick cooking spray.

2 In an electric mixer, beat together butter, sugar, egg, and vanilla extract.

3 Add flour, ground cinnamon, baking powder, and baking soda to the butter mixture and mix until all is combined into a thick dough. Knead in diced apples.

4 Place heaping tablespoon sized balls of cookie dough on the greased cookie sheets about 3 inches apart and press down to flatten.

5 Bake 14-15 minutes, just until the edges are golden brown. Let cool 10 minutes before serving.

Cushman's Tips

These are also very, very good when you add ½ cup of raisins to the dough at the end of step 3.

Apple Pie

TOTAL PREPARATION TIME: **1 ½ HRS**   DIFFICULTY: **MEDIUM**   SERVES: **8**

I don't need to tell you that something magical happens when you fill a pie crust with sliced apples, sugar, and spices! Though I now make this recipe with refrigerated pie crusts, the remainder is exactly how the Cushman family has been making this classic for generations.

Shopping List

1 stick butter
¼ cup all-purpose flour
¼ cup apple juice
½ cup sugar
½ cup light brown sugar
1 teaspoon vanilla extract
1 teaspoon apple pie spice
2 9-inch refrigerated pie crusts, thawed
4 cups peeled, cored, and sliced apples
1 large egg, beaten
coarse sugar, optional

1 Preheat oven to 425 degrees F. Heat butter in a saucepan over medium-high heat, until melted. Whisk in flour and cook 1 minute.

2 Add apple juice, sugar, brown sugar, vanilla extract, and apple pie spice to the butter and flour mixture, and bring up to a boil. Reduce heat to medium-low and let simmer 3 minutes.

3 Press 1 pie crust into the bottom of a 9-inch pie plate and pile ½ of the sliced apples over top. Pour ½ of the simmered liquid over the apples.

4 Toss remaining sliced apples with the remaining liquid and then pour over top of the apples in the pie. Do not be afraid to pile them high!

5 Cover pie with remaining crust, crimping edges to fuse the bottom and top crust together. Trim any excess crust from around the edges and cut slices in the top crust to vent. Lightly brush with beaten egg and sprinkle with coarse sugar (if desired).

6 Place pie in oven and then immediately reduce oven temperature to 350 degrees F. Bake 45-50 minutes, or until filling is bubbling and crust is browned. Let cool at least 15 minutes before slicing.

Cushman's Tips

For the best looking pie, lay the top crust out on a floured cutting board and use a pastry or pizza cutter to slice into 1-inch wide strips. Lay over pie in a criss-cross fashion to create a lattice top.

Cherry-Oh!! Cherries

Main Courses and Sides

Desserts

Cherry-Oh!!
CHERRIES

Slow Cooker Cherry Glazed Meatballs

TOTAL PREPARATION TIME: **5+ HRS**   DIFFICULTY: **EASY**   SERVES: **6**

These slow cooker meatballs with a sweet and savory cherry sauce make a great entrée over rice, but they are even better as a party appetizer. You can even put the whole slow cooker out at your party and keep them warm as you entertain!

Shopping List

MEATBALLS

2 pounds lean ground beef

2 large eggs

¼ cup breadcrumbs

¼ cup finely minced onion

½ teaspoon salt

¼ teaspoon garlic powder

SAUCE

2 cups cherries, pitted

1 ½ cups beef broth

3 tablespoons light brown sugar

½ cup ketchup

1 teaspoon cornstarch

1 In a large mixing bowl, combine all Meatball ingredients and form into golf ball-sized meatballs.

2 Place all Sauce ingredients in a slow cooker set to low and stir to combine.

3 Add meatballs to the sauce in the slow cooker, cover, and let cook 5-6 hours.

4 Remove meatballs, mash any whole cherries into the sauce, and then return meatballs to the pot to coat before serving.

Cushman's Tips

For the best flavor, season the sauce with salt to taste before serving. The salt will help enhance the sweet and tart flavors of the cherry sauce.

Cherry-Oh!!
CHERRIES

Ham Steaks with Cherry Dijon Sauce

TOTAL PREPARATION TIME: **25** MINS   DIFFICULTY: EASY   SERVES: **4**

Cherries and Dijon mustard are two things that go perfectly with a nice, cured ham steak. When all three are combined in the same dish, as they are in this one, some kitchen magic is going on!

Shopping List

2 large ham steaks

1 cup fresh cherries, pitted

½ cup water

2 tablespoons Dijon mustard

1 tablespoon light brown sugar

⅛ teaspoon onion powder

1 Preheat oven to 350 degrees F. Place ham steaks on a sheet pan and bake until warmed throughout, about 10-15 minutes.

2 Meanwhile, create the Cherry Dijon Sauce by placing all remaining ingredients in a sauce pot over medium heat. Cover and let simmer 8 minutes.

3 Use a potato masher or heavy spoon to mash cherries into the sauce. Let the mashed mixture simmer, uncovered, an additional 5 minutes before removing from heat.

4 Serve the baked ham steaks drizzled with the Cherry Dijon Sauce.

Cushman's Tips

*Y*ou can also grill the ham steaks on a traditional or indoor grill on high for about 3-5 minutes on each side.

Cherry-Oh!!
CHERRIES

Green Beans with Pistachios and Cherries

TOTAL PREPARATION TIME: 15 MINS   DIFFICULTY: EASY   SERVES: 4

These green beans are quickly made in the microwave with tangy orange zest, rich pistachios, and sweet, fresh cherries. The cherries cook up nice and soft and, once the final dish is stirred, almost cook into a sauce for the beans.

Shopping List

1 (16-ounce) bag frozen green beans

2 tablespoons butter or margarine

2 tablespoons water

⅛ teaspoon garlic powder

¼ teaspoon salt

⅛ teaspoon pepper

⅓ cup shelled pistachios

½ cup cherries, pitted and halved

1 teaspoon orange, tangerine, or HoneyBell zest

1 Place green beans, butter, water, garlic powder, salt, and pepper in a microwave-safe bowl and cover with plastic wrap. Poke a small hole in plastic wrap to vent.

2 Microwave on high for 5 minutes.

3 Remove plastic wrap and stir in pistachios, cherries, and HoneyBell zest. Return to microwave and heat on high 2 minutes or until green beans are hot throughout. Stir well before serving.

Cushman's Tips

I also like to make this with chopped hazelnuts in place of the pistachios, but I can't always find them available to purchase outside of a multiple nut mix.

Cherry Chunk Brownies

TOTAL PREPARATION TIME: 45 MINS   DIFFICULTY: EASY   SERVES: 9

I am kind of a brownie nut, especially when those brownies contain walnuts! Well, these brownies are not only chock-full of walnuts but also a good amount of fresh cherries too. It simply can't get any better than that!

Shopping List

nonstick cooking spray

1 stick butter or margarine, melted

1 cup sugar

2 large eggs

½ teaspoon vanilla extract

½ teaspoon pure almond extract

½ cup unsweetened cocoa powder

½ cup all-purpose flour

¼ teaspoon baking powder

½ cup chopped cherries

½ cup chopped walnuts

1 Preheat oven to 350 degrees F. Spray an 8x8 baking dish with nonstick cooking spray.

2 In an electric mixer, beat together melted butter, sugar, eggs, vanilla extract, and almond extract.

3 Add cocoa powder, flour, and baking powder to the mixture and beat for about 1 minute, or until all is well combined. Gently fold in chopped cherries and walnuts.

4 Pour batter into the greased baking dish and bake 25-30 minutes, or until the center is mostly set and only slightly jiggles when nudged with a potholder. Let cool at least 10 minutes before cutting into 9 squares.

Cushman's Tips

These are also very, very good when topped with the Cherry Cheese Frosting featured in the recipe for Devil's Food Cake with Cherry Cheese Frosting, recipe page: 203.

Cherry-Oh!!
CHERRIES

Homemade Cherry Pie

TOTAL PREPARATION TIME: 1 ½ HRS   DIFFICULTY: HARD   SERVES: 8

I don't know anyone that makes cherry pies from real cherries and not canned pie filling these days, but the difference in quality is worth the effort that you must put in to pit the cherries.

Shopping List

2 9-inch refrigerated pie crusts, thawed

1 teaspoon all-purpose flour

4 cups cherries, pitted

1 ¾ cups sugar

¼ cup plus 2 tablespoons all-purpose flour

1 tablespoon butter, melted

1 teaspoon pure almond extract

1 large egg, beaten

1 Preheat oven to 425 degrees F.

2 Press 1 pie crust into the bottom of a 9-inch pie plate and sprinkle the inside with 1 teaspoon of all-purpose flour.

3 In a large mixing bowl, combine cherries, sugar, flour, melted butter, and almond extract to create the filling.

4 Pour filling into the prepared crust and top with the second pie crust, trimming and crimping the edges to seal. Cut small slices in the top crust to vent and then lightly brush with beaten egg.

5 Place pie in oven and then immediately reduce oven temperature to 350 degrees F. Bake 45-50 minutes, or until filling is bubbling and crust is browned. Let cool at least 15 minutes before slicing.

Cushman's Tips

Using pure almond extract is a must in this recipe, as artificial almond extract has an entirely different taste.

Cherry-Oh!!
CHERRIES

Cherry and Rhubarb Cobbler

TOTAL PREPARATION TIME: 1 HOUR   **DIFFICULTY: MEDIUM**   **SERVES: 6**

Rhubarb is a bright red, stalky vegetable that is wonderfully tart in sweetened dishes like this Cherry and Rhubarb Cobbler. The tartness of the rhubarb really adds a nice dimension when you are using less tart dessert cherries like the Cherry-Oh!! variety.

Shopping List

nonstick cooking spray

2 cups cherries, pitted

3 cups rhubarb, chopped

1 cup sugar

2 tablespoons butter or margarine, melted

½ teaspoon vanilla extract

TOPPING

1 cup all-purpose flour

⅓ cup sugar

4 tablespoons butter or margarine, chilled

½ teaspoon ground cinnamon

1 Preheat oven to 400 degrees F. Spray an 8x8 baking dish with nonstick cooking spray.

2 In a large mixing bowl, combine cherries, rhubarb, sugar, butter, and vanilla extract, and pour into the greased baking dish.

3 In a food processor, combine all Topping ingredients, pulsing until combined and crumbly. Drop by the large spoonful over top of the fruit mixture in the baking dish.

4 Bake for 25-30 minutes, or until bubbly hot and topping has begun to brown. Let cool for at least 5 minutes before spooning into serving bowls.

Cushman's Tips

You can also make this a cherry-only cobbler by simply skipping the rhubarb and using 5 total cups of pitted cherries.

Chocolate Covered Cherries

TOTAL PREPARATION TIME: 4 HRS   **DIFFICULTY: HARD**   **SERVES: 12**

Chocolate covered cherries made from real, fresh cherries, especially sweet dessert ones like Chery-Oh!! Cherries, are an absolute treat that is sure to impress guests or friends.

Shopping List

24-36 cherries

toothpicks

1 cup corn syrup

¼ teaspoon pure almond extract

1 (12-ounce) bag semi-sweet chocolate chips

1 Line a sheet pan with parchment paper.

2 Remove cherry stems and then pit each cherry. Stick each cherry with a toothpick.

3 In a bowl, combine corn syrup and almond extract. Dip each cherry in corn syrup mixture and then set on parchment paper to dry. Let dry, uncovered, at least 4 hours.

4 Line a second sheet pan with parchment paper. Place chocolate chips in a metal or tempered-glass mixing bowl and place over a pot of simmering water to create a double boiler.

5 Stir the chocolate chips constantly, until entirely melted.

6 Dip the corn syrup covered cherries into the melted chocolate and then place onto the lined sheet pan to cool. Let cool completely before removing toothpicks and serving.

Cushman's Tips

Once you've melted the chocolate, it is important to work very fast or it will harden before you can get all of the cherries covered.

Cherry-Oh!!
CHERRIES

Cherry and Pineapple Fluff

TOTAL PREPARATION TIME: 15 MINS   **DIFFICULTY: EASY**   **SERVES: 8**

This is a simple and great potluck dish because it is cool, refreshing, and most likely to be different from all of the other dishes at the party. A creamy parfait-style dessert with chopped cherries, crushed pineapple, pecans, and miniature marshmallows folded into whipped cream, this dessert is also a huge hit with kids.

Shopping List

1 ½ cups cherries, pitted and chopped

1 (20-ounce) can crushed pineapple, drained

1 cup chopped pecans

1 (12-ounce) tub non-dairy whipped topping, thawed

1 cup miniature marshmallows

1 In a large bowl, combine cherries, pineapple, and pecans.

2 Gently fold in non-dairy whipped topping and miniature marshmallows, until all is well combined. Serve immediately.

Cushman's Tips

Be careful not to over-stir the whipped topping as you incorporate it into the other ingredients or it may lose its air and turn to liquid.

Cherry Dessert and Pancake Sauce

TOTAL PREPARATION TIME: 25 MINS   DIFFICULTY: EASY   SERVES: 24

This real Cherry Dessert and Pancake Sauce makes the perfect topping for ice cream sundaes, pancakes and French toast, cheesecakes, or even just vanilla yogurt!

Shopping List

3 cups cherries, pitted

½ cup sugar

1 teaspoon lemon juice

¼ teaspoon pure almond extract, optional (see my tips)

1 ½ teaspoons cornstarch

½ cup water

1 Add cherries, sugar, lemon juice, and almond extract to a sauce pot over medium-high heat.

2 Whisk cornstarch into the water until fully combined. Stir into the cherry mixture on the stove and cook, stirring constantly, until bubbling hot. Reduce heat to low and let cook 4 minutes.

3 Using a potato masher or heavy spoon, roughly crush about half of the cherries into the sauce and continue cooking an additional 2 minutes. Remove from heat and let cool.

4 Serve warm or chilled.

Cushman's Tips

The almond extract is completely optional, but I find that it greatly enhances the flavor of fresh cherries. Cherries and almonds come from the same family, so you will find that "pure" almond extract actually smells exactly like cherries!

Cherry Mousse

TOTAL PREPARATION TIME: 20 MINS   DIFFICULTY: EASY   SERVES: 8

Making real, light and fluffy homemade mousse desserts couldn't be any easier! In fact, the only reason I gave this recipe a preparation time of "20 minutes" is to allot time for pitting the fresh cherries. Once you've gotten that out of the way, you can literally whip up a batch in only 2 minutes!

Shopping List

2 cups cherries, pitted

⅛ teaspoon almond extract

2 cups heavy cream

2 tablespoons confectioners' sugar

1 In a food processor, purée cherries and almond extract until mostly smooth.

2 Using an electric mixer, whip the cream and sugar until solid peaks form.

3 Gently fold puréed cherry mixture into the whipped cream to create the mousse. Serve immediately.

Cushman's Tips

For the best presentation, serve in wine or martini glasses, garnished with a fresh or maraschino cherry.

Cherry-Oh!!
CHERRIES

Cherry Cream Cake

TOTAL PREPARATION TIME: 1 ½ HRS   DIFFICULTY: EASY   SERVES: 8

I like making desserts from store-bought cake mixes because it allows me to get creative in the kitchen with only about half of the work of starting from scratch. Without that luxury I'm not sure if I would have ever taken the time to come up with this great recipe for a creamy, fresh cherry filled cake.

Shopping List

nonstick cooking spray

1 (18.25-ounce) box yellow cake mix

3 large eggs

1 cup water

⅓ cup vegetable oil

8 ounces light sour cream

¾ teaspoon pure almond extract

¼ teaspoon salt

1 cup fresh cherries, pitted and chopped

1 Preheat oven to 350 degrees F. Spray a bundt pan with nonstick cooking spray.

2 In an electric mixer, combine yellow cake mix, eggs, water, vegetable oil, sour cream, almond extract, and salt. Beat until smooth and creamy, about 2 minutes.

3 Fold chopped cherries into the cake batter and pour into the greased bundt pan.

4 Bake 50-60 minutes, or until a toothpick inserted into the center comes out mostly clean. Let cool before slicing.

Cushman's Tips

This is really good when drizzled with chocolate syrup before serving. I like the standard chocolate syrup (like Hershey's).

Baked Banana Split Squares

TOTAL PREPARATION TIME: 1 HOUR   **DIFFICULTY: MEDIUM**   **SERVES: 9**

These chewy, blondie-like cookie bars have the classic flavors of an old-fashioned banana split! With mashed bananas and whole cherries baked into the batter and a homemade chocolate icing drizzle, the only thing missing is a brain-freeze!

Shopping List

nonstick cooking spray

1 stick butter or margarine, melted

2 small bananas, peeled and mashed

1 cup light brown sugar

½ cup sugar

1 large egg, beaten

2 teaspoons vanilla extract

1 ½ cups all-purpose flour

1 ½ teaspoons baking powder

1 ¼ cups cherries, pitted

CHOCOLATE ICING

1 cup confectioners sugar

1 ½ tablespoons milk

1 tablespoon unsweetened cocoa powder

1 Preheat oven to 350 degrees F. Spray an 8x8 baking dish with nonstick cooking spray.

2 In an electric mixer, combine butter, mashed banana, brown sugar, sugar, egg, and vanilla extract.

3 Add flour and baking powder to the mixture and beat for about 1 minute, or until all is combined. Gently fold in cherries.

4 Pour batter into the greased baking dish and bake 40-45 minutes, or until a toothpick inserted into the center comes out mostly clean. Let cool at least 5 minutes before cutting into 9 squares.

5 In a microwave-safe bowl, combine all Icing ingredients and microwave 30 seconds, just until mixture is smooth and somewhat thin. Drizzle evenly over the baked squares and let cool an additional 5 minutes. Serve warm or at room temperature.

Cushman's Tips

For even more of that classic banana split flavor, you can also add ⅓ cup of chopped peanuts to the batter in step 3.

Cherry-Oh!! CHERRIES

Devil's Food Cake with Cherry Cheese Frosting

TOTAL PREPARATION TIME: **1** HOUR   DIFFICULTY: MEDIUM   SERVES: **12**

With a mixture of a store-bought devil's food cake mix and a fresh, homemade Cherry Cream Cheese Frosting, this cake is a breeze to make and a unique treat that you can't find anywhere else!

Shopping List

1 (18.25-ounce) box devil's food cake mix

3 large eggs

1 cup water

⅓ cup vegetable oil

½ cup fresh cherries, pitted and puréed

white chocolate chips, optional, for garnish

toasted almonds, optional, for garnish

chocolate cookies, optional, for garnish

FROSTING

8 ounces cream cheese, softened

1 stick butter, softened

¾ teaspoon vanilla extract

½ teaspoon pure almond extract

6 fresh cherries, pitted and puréed

1 (16-ounce) box confectioners sugar

1 Preheat oven to 350 degrees F. In an electric mixer, combine cake mix, eggs, water, vegetable oil, and fresh puréed cherries. Beat until smooth and creamy, about 2 minutes.

2 Pour cake batter into 2 greased 8-inch cake pans and bake 30-35 min-utes, or until a toothpick inserted into the center comes out mostly clean. Let cool completely.

3 With an electric mixer, create the Frosting by beating together cream cheese and butter until creamy. Add va-nilla extract, almond extract, and fresh puréed cherries and beat until combined.

4 Slowly beat in confectioners sugar until all is combined and a thick Frosting has formed. Refrigerate for 30 minutes to harden.

5 Spread a layer of frosting between the two layers of cake, and then frost the entire outside surface of the cake. Sprin-kle with white chocolate chips and toast-ed almonds for garnish. Arrange cookies along the bottom of the cake for decora-tion (as pictured at left). Slice and serve!

Cushman's Tips

You can also make this into a 4-layer cake by using a long cake knife to cut each of the 2 cakes in half before spread-ing the frosting.

Allen Cushman

In 1945, *Allen Cushman*'s father, Ed Cushman, opened a small citrus store in West Palm Beach, Florida. From the very beginning, Cushman's Fruit Company was a family affair dedicated to shipping wonderful Florida citrus all around the country. When Allen and his brothers Mike and John were old enough, they began pitching in at the store on weekends and throughout the summers. As they grew older, they joined their father in the business full-time.

Giving Florida's visitors the opportunity to send a taste of their travels home was a novel idea that gave Cushman's Fruit Company its start, but it was the taste of one fruit in particular that made Cushman's a household name.

The HoneyBell is a spectacularly sweet and juicy cross between a Dancy tangerine and a Duncan grapefruit. While the Cushman family didn't invent the fruit, it was Allen's father Ed that coined the name—HoneyBell—after its sweet taste and unique bell shape.

More than half a century later, the humble Cushman's citrus store has grown quite a bit. Now a proud part of the Harry and David family, Allen Cushman is helping to spread the joy of Cushman's HoneyBells and other high-quality fruit to more people than ever.

You can still visit the
Cushman's Fruit Company retail store at:

204 US Highway 1
North Palm Beach, FL

To order Cushman's high quality fruit and gourmet gifts, visit them online at:

www.HoneyBell.com

Recipe Index

HoneyBells

Crown Ruby Red Grapefruits

Honeycrisp Apples

Cherry-Oh!! Cherries

TO ORDER THE
HIGHEST QUALITY FRUIT
AND GOURMET GIFTS,
PLEASE VISIT US
ONLINE AT

www.HoneyBell.com